Paddling Around Nashville

37 Kayaking and Canoeing Trips in Middle Tennessee

Paddling Around Nashville

37 Kayaking and Canoeing Trips in Middle Tennessee

Patty Shultz

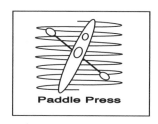

Paddle Press

Shultz, Patty.
    Paddling around Nashville: 37kayaking and canoeing trips in middle Tennessee / Patty Shultz. — 1st ed.
    p. cm.
    Includes bibliographical references.
    LCCN 2005900235
    ISBN 0-9764568-0-X

    1. Canoes and canoeing—Tennessee—Nashville Region—Guidebooks. 2. Nashville Region (Tenn.)—Guidebooks.
    I. Title.

GV776.T22N37 2005   797.1'22'0976855
                                        QBI05-200023

Printed in the United States of America
Published by Paddle Press

Paddle Press
709 Roantree Dr
Brentwood, TN 37027

This guide cannot be expected to replace appropriate courses or training in paddling. The ultimate responsibility for safety lies with the reader.

Dedication

This book is dedicated to Ned
who supported this endeavor from start to finish

And to Carolyne, Mary and Alice
who were involved in the adventure every Wednesday

Acknowledgments

Thanks to Carolyne Goddard, Mary Coffee and Alice Rotan for the adventure of exploring the waterways in Middle Tennessee.

Thanks to Matt Orozco for teaching me Illustrator, Quark and Photoshop, so I could get this book ready for printing. Thanks to Susan Fitzhenry for editorial assistance. Thanks to Heloise Shilstat, John McFadden, Marshall Spencer and Skip Hindman for previewing the text. Thanks to Mack Pritchard and Fran Wallas for advice.

Thanks to Mimi of Mimi's Bookmarks for designing a great paddling bookmark.

Thanks to Tennessee Scenic Rivers Association and the Watershed Associations for their efforts to save the rivers, teach classes and keep us involved with the great water resources in Middle Tennessee.

Thanks to local canoe outfitters willing to talk rivers, paddlers willing to share favorite spots and friends who joined in paddling trips.

Thanks to Betsy Mayers and Holly Sherwin, two authors on paddling, who shared their experiences and advice.

And a special thank you to my family: Rainbow for the encouragement and painted paddle, Ted for computer help, Forest for paddling and the inspiration of going out on a limb, Beck for joining on trips and the logo, my mom for always reading and writing and most of all Ned for supporting this project on all levels!

Foreword

by Marshall Spencer
Past President of Tennessee Scenic Rivers
Associations

Tennessee's abundance of creeks, rivers, and lakes is renowned. And Middle Tennessee has much to offer for the paddler who wishes to spend a day exploring local waterways. Originating in the forested hills of the Highland Rim, rivers and creeks flow in a wide variety of sizes and topographies. They fascinated me after I moved to Hickman County from Minnesota 15 years ago, compelling me to explore what lay around the next bend in each river. My explorations have never ceased. There are so many places to paddle, particularly if one is not picky about putting up with the occasional stretch of shallow water and portages around fallen trees. Some of the features of these places change from month-to-month, season-to-season, and year-to-year. There is always some beauty to find in each trip, and the journeys are often enchanting.

Armed with a good map, information provided by local residents and frequent visitors, and a reliable guidebook, the paddler who loves to explore will find new places and challenges for many years. I wish this book had been available when I first started looking for places to paddle in the Nashville area.

It was through the Tennessee Scenic Rivers Association – usually referred to as TSRA – that I came to know Patty and many others who share my passion for running rivers. TSRA members like to paddle and are a great resource for information and instruction about where to paddle and how to do it safely. This nonprofit, all-volunteer organization is a leader in working to conserve and protect Tennessee's rivers and lakes. Awareness of opportunities to enjoy the high quality of our rivers, creeks, and lakes is a first step toward preserving these resources. This guidebook will help you get started or will add to your knowledge of paddling opportunities within a two-hour drive of Nashville. I hope you will use it to find those special places where clear water flows among the hills, cascades over limestone stair steps, and meanders at the foot of tall bluffs crowned with red cedar trees.

Comments by John McFadden
Director, Science and Restorations Programs
TSRA's Duck River Opportunities Project
Director, Science and Restoration Programs
Harpeth River Watershed Association

For me, it is an inherently spiritual activity to glide across the lake water and to pass seemingly effortlessly through the splash of rapids or the gentle currents of flat waters. To be on the water as the sun rises or sets is to watch the hand of the Creator do His most magnificent of work! To recreate in this hurried society is to re-create our spiritual, emotional and physical selves.

Protecting these resources has been the focus of my career, yet as Edward Abby said - working to protect those resources is NOT enough - we MUST get out and enjoy them!

Patty Shultz has given us a great guide to enjoying some of the aquatic natural resources in the middle Tennessee area. I encourage you and your family to float Bledsoe Creek, paddle the still waters of Percy Priest and look for mussels on the Duck River. Reach out and enjoy this wondrous thing we call creation. After all, it is our home!

Contents

Section 3 – Creek Trips

Introduction

The purpose of this book is to share paddling places around Nashville. Moving to Nashville 8 years ago, I had a hard time finding paddling put ins and take outs other than the notorious and beautiful Narrows of the Harpeth. So with maps in hand, my paddling friends and I began exploring local areas that looked like they had potential. We became aware of great organizations like the TSRA (Tennessee Scenic Rivers Association) and the HRWA (Harpeth River Watershed Association). For classes, safety information and more, check out the TSRA web site at www.paddletsra.com. Along the way, we met other paddlers who shared great spots. After a while, we became familiar with a number of awesome trips that weren't all that well known. I wanted to write them down to share with others. Here is the result. Enjoy the adventures.

Middle Tennessee has an extraordinary number of beautiful spots for paddling. These aren't the fast paced, high adrenaline waterways of Eastern Tennessee fame. Instead, they offer more cautious outdoor adventures and opportunities to commune with nature. Fortunately, another great feature of these trips is that they are right outside our back door! It is to be hoped that as more of us become aware of these treasures, more of us will be willing to protect them.

This book is divided into **3 sections**: lakes, rivers and creeks.

Theoretically, the **lakes** are the calmest and offer the beginner a place to learn basic skills in a safe environment. Both J Percy Priest and Old Hickory are massive bodies of water with multiple spots for enjoying the great outdoors. Assuming that you are already wearing a life jacket, motorboats are the biggest safety concern. Stay alert and out of the way of moterboats.

The **rivers** in this book offer a nice progression for the beginning paddler. They are generally wide with a gentle current. The width allows for more leeway in moving one's boat downstream as the current assists the paddling. However, the safety concerns increase. Obstacles in the river like deadfalls and strainers are to be avoided. Stay as far from these as possible as the water pressure through these can be intense, trapping objects like boats and people while the water runs freely through. The other major concern is flood stage water flows. After heavy rains, the usually calm Middle Tennessee rivers can rage and are unsafe.

The **creeks** in this book require more expertise in paddling skills. Narrow chutes and deadfalls require more precise maneuvers. Often portaging is required around deadfalls. The remote nature of many of the creeks requires a reliance on partner paddlers in case of mishaps. Good safety practices are a must.

A note on format

Directions are all from Nashville. Take out locations are given first, as one usually wants to leave a car at take out for shuttling purposes. Put in locations are listed second. Depending on one's individual preference in shuttle routine this can be modified.

Each paddle trip section has a reference to a Map and number. This corresponds to the pages and map numbers in the <u>Tennessee Atlas & Gazetteer</u>, seventh Edition, DeLorme. 2004.

Safety

Water adventures require attention be paid to safety.

Some considerations to be mindful of:

1. Know your **paddling skills** and your limits.
2. Always a wear safety **personal flotation device** (pfd).
3. Be aware of water hazards and avoid them or deal appropriately with them:
   a. **High Water**, following heavy rains or following dam releases, can result in river current that is overwhelming and dangerous. This situation is likely to create new deadfalls with heavy current running against them. Avoid paddling when water is in flood stage.
   b. **Cold water** and cold weather can lead to hypothermia. Take along a dry bag with a change of clothing.
   c. **Strainers** are anything in the river that lets water flow through but pins boats and boaters against it – most commonly deadfalls. The water pressure against anything trapped in the strainer can be very dangerous and deadly.
   d. **Dams** cause the water falling over them to curl backward and create an action that traps a boat or boater in a wave. If trapped, go deep to where water is flowing downstream or swim out the end of the wave. Better yet avoid dams.
4. Proper equipment is essential. See that your boat and paddles are in good repair. Also take along a whistle, first aid kit, safety rope and drinking water.
5. Paddle with others; the usual recommendation is at least 3 boats.
6. Watch out for motorized boats on lakes or in deep channels of rivers and avoid them.

7. Keep tuned to the weather; storms and high winds can be dangerous.
8. Learn as much as you can about the water trip prior to heading out. A map is always helpful to assess where you are.

Disclaimer

This book is designed to provide directions for paddling trips around Nashville in Middle Tennessee. Despite the fact that we have paddled all the runs in this book and found them safe, one must be aware that conditions change. It is up to the individual paddler to be sure the trip is right for him or her and to avoid dangers. Variations in water level, deadfalls and other natural surprises make each trip unique.

Every effort has been made to make this manual as accurate as possible. However, there may be mistakes in type or content. Furthermore some information may be accurate only up to printing time. Therefore, this book should be used only as a guide.

The purpose of this guide is to share paddling trips and to offer entertainment for others interested in water outings. The author and Paddle Press Publishing shall have neither liability nor responsibility to any person or entity with respect to any loss of property, well being, inconvenience or damage caused, or alleged to have been caused, directly or indirectly, by the information contained in this text. If you do not wish to be bound by the above, you may return this book to Paddle Press for a full refund.

Access Issues

There is a body of Federal Law, along with Supreme Court decisions, confirming the right to paddle on rivers and streams. However, be aware that there are a few landowners who do not accept this. Local sentiment varies. Occasionally, you may run into barbed wire strung across the stream, or people concerned about you paddling through their private property.

There is no right to cross private land to get to a river. But the courts have ruled that when one public route crosses or meets another public route (e.g. a highway and a river) there is a right of passage. So access is possible at bridges, as long as you stay on the states right of way along the bridge.

For further reference and more information on river law, check out the National Organization of Rivers website at www.nationalrivers.org.

In this book, where there is public parking, it is noted. However, there are places where "posted" signs appear near the put in or take out. Use caution where parking, to access the water. The land that the state or local county owns, for right of way, varies from road to road. If the land around put in and take out is private, you should pleasantly request use of the land to park for a paddling trip. We have never been denied access when we asked but often hear stories of groups that litter and don't respect the land. It is a good idea to carry a trash bag, so that you can leave the area in better condition than you found it.

Lake Trips

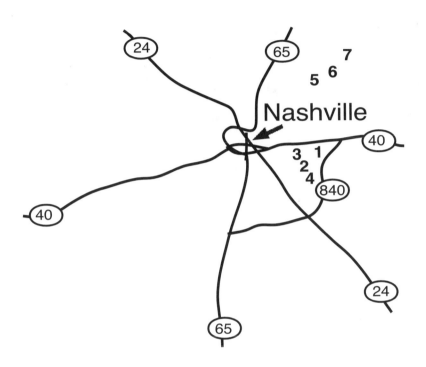

1. J Percy Priest - Vivrett Creek Area
2. J Percy Priest - Stewarts Creek
3. J Percy Priest - Finch Branch
4. J Percy Priest - Jefferson Springs Public Use Area
5. Old Hickory Lake - Lone Branch on Cedar Creek
6. Old Hickory Lake - Riverview Access on Spencer Creek
7. Old Hickory Lake - Old Union Access on Bledsoe Creek

Lakes, as still water, offer a great place to begin paddling. Learn your skills in a safe environment wearing a personal floatation device. Avoid motorboats.

J Percy Priest

In 1970, the TVA finished the dam on the Stones River resulting in the creation of the J Percy Priest Lake. This massive water body covers 14,000 acres and offers many recreational options. The first time I set out canoeing here, I went in by a motorboat marina and felt like a bicycle on an L.A. expressway: Since then, I've learned of quieter locations and areas where there are "no-wake" zones. This is much more pleasant for the paddler.

Paddle # 1 Vivrett Creek

Located on the eastern side of J Percy Priest Lake, the Vivrett Public Use Access Area is a jewel with a parking lot right next to an easy put in. Lack of on water facilities here, a large no wake zone and shallow water discourage motorized traffic in this area. Besides exploring the cove area, there are three creeks that join the lake in this area. Paddling up the creeks has a very remote feel. Then if you want to flex your muscles or explore, the great expanses of the lake area are ideal.

Directions to Put In and Take Out

From Nashville, head east on Interstate 40 to Exit 221 B for Old Hickory Blvd.
At exit turn right (south) onto Old Hickory Blvd.
Continue on Old Hickory Blvd for 0.5 miles to Bell Rd.
Turn left (east) on Bell Rd.
Continue on Bell Rd for 0.6 miles to until it ends on S New Hope Rd.
Turn right on S New Hope Rd.
Continue on S New Hope Rd for 1.2 miles to until it ends on Stewarts Ferry Rd.
Turn left (east) on Stewarts Ferry Rd.
Proceed on Stewarts Ferry Rd for 1.0 mile.

Turn left (north east) onto Sperry Rd.

Continue on Sperry Rd for 1.7 miles to the entrance for the Vivrett Public Use Area.

Turn right into the drive – a brown sign identifies the area.

The parking area is 0.3 miles down the drive.

Put In and Take Out Access

Access is very easy and convenient with the paved parking lot right next to the lake. There is also a boat ramp right into the lake.

Precautions

Avoid motorized boats and strong winds on open waters.

Map

TN Atlas Map 53

Paddling in Vivrett Creek

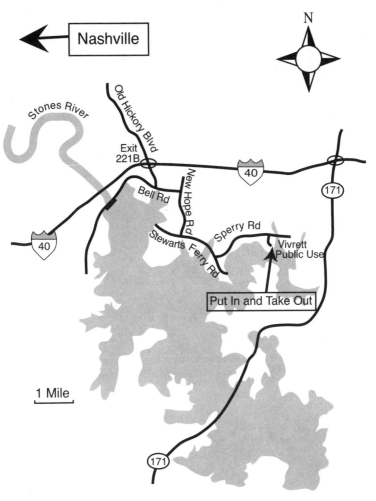

J Percy Priest

Vivrett Creek Public Use Access

Paddle #1

J.Percy Priest

Stewarts Creek Boat Use Area for Stewarts Creek and Finch Creek

Located on the southwestern side of J. Percy Priest Lake, this access area is provided by the US Army Corps of Engineers. There are two parking lots, one with a boat ramp right into the lake. This access area is also ideal for the motorized boat so you do have to be cautious on hot summer weekends. There is a channel deep enough for the motorboats, but if you stick to the sides, the water is less than 10 feet and it's yours.

Paddle #2 Stewarts Creek

As you face the lake from the launch area, Stewarts Creek is to your left. If you stay close to shore and bear left (heading south), you will be in Stewarts Creek. The terrain along the banks shifts from rocky shore to woods. There are number of places good for a swim or picnic. For the first mile of paddling, the northwestern bank is a Wildlife Management Area.

Paddle #3 Finch Branch

While Stewarts Creek heads south and is easy to follow, Finch Branch is a little harder to identify. About a mile down from the Stewarts Creek dock, bearing off to the west, is the Finch Branch. For over a mile, this creek has Wildlife Management Area land on both banks, and without a deep channel beyond its entrance, it's not of as much interest to the motorboats. The birds in this area are awesome.

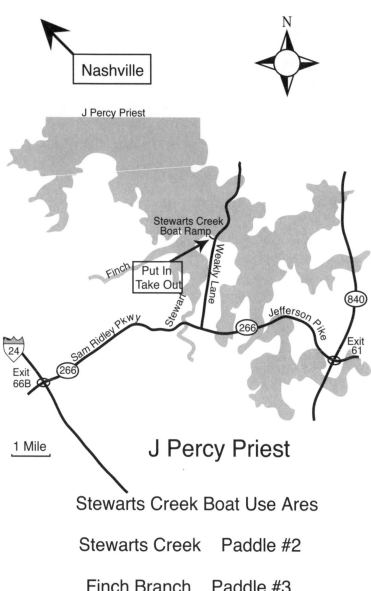

Nashville

J Percy Priest

Stewarts Creek
Boat Ramp

Finch

Put In
Take Out

Weakly Lane

Stewart

Sam Ridley Pkwy

Jefferson Pike

840

266

Exit
61

24

Exit
66B

266

1 Mile

J Percy Priest

Stewarts Creek Boat Use Ares

Stewarts Creek   Paddle #2

Finch Branch   Paddle #3

Directions to Put In and Take Out

From Nashville, head east on Interstate 24 toward
    Chattanooga.
Take Interstate 24 to exit 66B for Sam Ridley Parkway
    heading east (Hwy 266).
Go on Sam Ridley Parkway for 4.7 miles to Weakley Lane.
Turn left onto Weakley Lane.
Proceed on Weakley Lane for 2.3 miles to the entrance of
    the Stewarts Creek Boat Ramp Use.
Turn left into the boat use area and follow the road to the
    parking areas and ramp.

Put In and Take Out Access

Access is very easy and convenient with the paved parking lot right next to the lake. The boat ramp goes right into
the lake if you find that to be a desirable feature.

Precautions

Avoid motorized boats and strong winds on open waters.

Map TN Atlas Map 53

Paddling Percy Priest

J Percy Priest

Paddle #4 Jefferson Springs Recreation Access

Located in the south west corner of Percy Priest Lake about 2 miles above the junction of the west and east forks of the Stones River is the Jefferson Springs Recreation Area. This area was created by the US Army Corps of Engineers and has three parking lots, a park and a boat ramp. The park is worth noting because of its many picnic tables and grills nestled under a canopy of trees as well as a gazebo, all with a view of the lake. The channel does run through the lake here so there are motor boats to deal with, but the banks have water levels less than 10 feet deep so you should be safe there.

East and West Forks of the Stones River

Facing the lake from the boat ramp, the forks of the river are to your right (south). As you paddle along, the banks offer a variety of views and wildlife. Unfortunately there is also trash left along the favorite stopping spots. This is a place where you might want to carry a trash bag to pick up a few things as you enjoy the deer in the woods, heron in the sky and fish jumping in the water.

Directions to Put In and Take Out

From Nashville, head east on Interstate 24 toward Chattanooga.

Take Interstate 24 to exit 66B for Sam Ridley Parkway heading east (Hwy 266).

Proceed on Sam Ridley Parkway for 5 miles to Jefferson Pike (266 North) traffic light.

At Jefferson Pike, turn left (heading east) continuing on Hwy 266 North.

Proceed on Jefferson Pike for 1.1 miles to the entrance on the left to the Jefferson Springs Recreation Area.

Access for Put In and Take Out

The far parking lot is in close proximity to the lake and has a boat ramp; both of these features make it very easy and convenient to access the water.

Precautions

Avoid motorized boats and strong winds on the open lake.

Map

TN Atlas Map 38

Cave-like rock structures are along J Percy Priest bank by the Jefferson Springs Public Use Area.

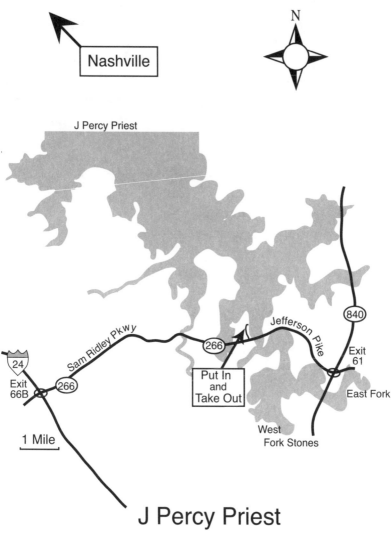

J Percy Priest

Jefferson Springs Recreation Area

Paddle #4

Old Hickory Lake

The Old Hickory Dam on the Cumberland River by the US Army Corps of Engineers avails us of 22,500 water acres in Old Hickory Lake. According to their report, there are also 12,200 land acres available for recreation. These acres are harder to find though, as much of the land around this lake is built up. Many homes with private boat docks adorn the banks. There are 65 recreation areas around Old Hickory Lake and 56 boat ramps, but most of these are dominated by motorboat traffic. In fact, I was cautioned by a ranger about paddling in the main channel of the Cumberland on weekends, because of the motorized traffic as well as barges. Further upstream from Hendersonville, there are a number of spots worth mentioning.

North of Mount Juliet

Two areas here are the **Lone Branch Access** on Cedar Creek and **Riverview Access** on Spencer Creek.

The Lone Branch Access is on a tree-lined cove with an adjacent park. If you are into easy paddling with young ones and a picnic, this might be a good spot for you. However, there is a marina and yacht club nearby which signals the presence of motorboats on sunny weekends. There are many tables with grills along with a picnic shelter, which can be reserved. Signs warn that swimming is at your own risk.

The Riverview Access on Spencer Creek is a beautiful spot. It's a slightly further drive up the road but probably worth it for the trade off of less traffic. Facing the water from the dock if you head right (south), you will be going to the source of Spencer Creek (rather than the Channel of the Cumberland). This area has a few houses and private docks in coves, but the majority of the banks are tree lined or farmland.

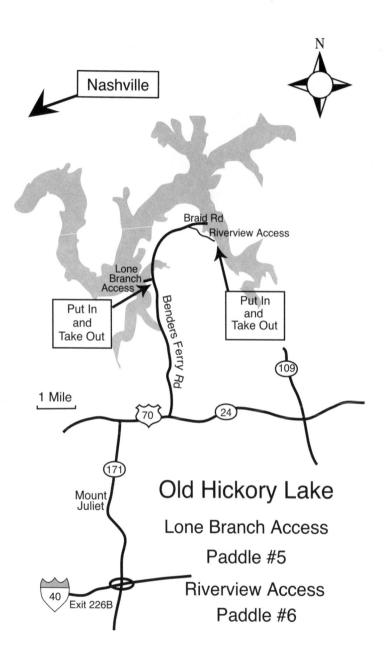

N

Nashville

Braid Rd
Riverview Access

Lone
Branch
Access

Put In
and
Take Out

Put In
and
Take Out

Benders Ferry Rd

109

1 Mile

70

24

171

Mount
Juliet

40

Exit 226B

Old Hickory Lake

Lone Branch Access

Paddle #5

Riverview Access

Paddle #6

Directions to Put In and Take Out

Paddle #5 Lone Branch Access

From Nashville, head east on Interstate 40.
Take Interstate 40 to Exit 226B north for Mt Juliet (Rt 171).
Proceed on Rt 171 through Mt Juliet for 4.3 miles until it
ends on Rt 70.
At the light intersection of Rt 171 and Rt 70, turn right
(east).
Proceed on Rt 70 for 1.1 miles to Benders Ferry Rd.
Turn left (north) onto Benders Ferry Rd.
Stay on Benders Ferry Rd for 3.7 miles to the sign on left for
Lone Branch Access.

Paddle #6 Riverview Access

Use above directions but continue on Benders Ferry Rd.
Go past Lone Branch Access for 1.7 miles to dead-end sign.
Go straight (off Benders Ferry Rd) on Braid Rd (dead end).
On Braid Rd for 0.5 miles until it ends in the parking lot for
the Riverview Access

Access for Put In and Take Out

Both the Lone Branch and the Riverview Access have boat
ramps right off the paved parking lots, which make them
very convenient for water use.

Precautions

Avoid motorized boats and strong winds on open waters.

Map

TN Atlas Map 54

Old Hickory Lake

Paddle #7 Bledsoe Creek Area

Bledsoe Creek runs from north to south in Sumner County. Below Rt 25, there is a channel, which makes it accessible to motorboats, but north of Rt 25, the slack water is rather shallow and paddlers are likely have the area to themselves. For the adventurous, see the description of the Bledsoe Creek Run from Rogana Rd to Rt 25 on page 105. If the water is low or you are interested in a put in and take out from the same place, this may be for you. There are a number of put ins on Bledsoe Creek, but the Old Union Access offers access to the more remote and less developed areas.

Old Union Access

From Nashville, head east on Interstate 40.
Take Interstate 40 to Exit 232B north to Gallatin (Rt 109).
Proceed north on Rt 109 for 12.8 miles to the light at
    Airport Rd.
Turn right (east) on Airport Rd.
Continue on Airport Rd for 3.8 miles to the light for Rt 25
    (also known as Hartsville Pike).
Turn right (east) on Hartsville Pike (Rt 25).
Proceed on Rt 25 for 3.2 miles approaching the bridge,
    which crosses Bledsoe Creek.
Before the bridge, note the road leading down to a parking
    area and turn right (south) here.
This is the Old Union Access.

Access for Put In and Take Out

The Old Union Access has a paved parking area and a boat ramp, which makes it very convenient for water use.

Precautions

Avoid motorized boats and strong winds on open waters.

Interesting Points

There is an orchard just east of the creek and the farm stand on Rt 25 just over the bridge offers fruit, cold drinks and homemade fried fruit pies.

Further south on the Bledsoe Creek is the Bledsoe Creek Camping State Park. This can be accessed by boat or going south on Zieglers Fort Rd which is about a mile west of the Old Union Access, off Rt 25.

Map

TN Atlas Map 54

A boating lunch on stillwater

Old Hickory Lake

Bledsoe Creek Area - Old Union Access

Paddle #7

Lake Trips

River Trips

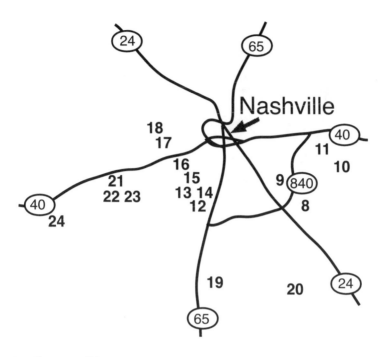

8. Stones River, West Fork - Thompson Lane to Nice Mill
9. Stones River, West Fork - Nice Mill to West Fork Ramp
10. Stones River, East Fork - Trimble Rd to G James Rd
11. Stones River, East Fork - Walter Hill to Mona Ramp
12. Harpeth River - Lewisburg Pike to Franklin Rec Center
13. Harpeth River - Del Rio Pike to Old Natchez Trace
14. Harpeth River - Old Natchez Trace to Moran Rd
15. Harpeth River - Old Natchez Trace to Hwy 100
16. Harpeth River - Hwy 100 to Newsome Station Mill
17. Harpeth River - Rt 249 to Cedar Hill Rd
18. Harpeth River - Narrows of the Harpeth
19. Duck River - Normandy Dam to Three Bridge Fork Rd
20. Duck River - Rt 99/431 to Carpenter Bridge Rd
21. Piney River - Interstate 40 to Piney River Rd
22. Piney River - Piney River Rd to Walter Nunnely Bridge
23. Piney River - Brook to Piney River Canoe and Camp
24. Buffalo River-Standing Rock Bridge to Blue Hole Bridge

Rivers here usually have a gentle current. However, following heavy rains or in wet seasons these same calm rivers can be dangerous. Generally they are wide enough to avoid the occasional deadfall. Paddling skills are needed here for safety.

Rocky ledges enhance many river excursions.

The Stones River

The East Fork, the West Fork and its tributary, the Middle Fork of the Stones River, join in Old Jefferson southeast of the impoundment for the J Percy Priest Lake. The Stones River flows through Rutherford and Davidson counties. After it leaves the J Percy Priest Dam, the Stones continues on to join the Cumberland River in Neelys Bend.

The Stones River system offers many opportunities for paddling, fishing and swimming.

Stones River West Fork

Paddle #8 Thompson Lane Greenway to Nice Mill Dam Site

This section of the West Fork is snappy and fast flowing at times. There is some development along this section with houses along the banks, but this makes an interesting contrast with the wilder sections. There are plenty of tree lined banks and awesome rock formations.

Directions to Take Out

From Nashville, head south on Interstate 65 to Exit 59 for 840 East (or east on Interstate 24 to Exit 74B for 840 East towards Knoxville).
Take 840 east to Exit #57 for Sulphur Spring Rd.
At the exit turn left (west) on Sulphur Springs Rd.
Take Sulphur Springs Rd for 1.8 miles to the second parking lot for Nice Mill Dam just after the Albert Gore Jr Bridge.

Take Out Access

There are parking lots on both sides of the Nice Mill

Dam, but the one on the north side (after the Albert Gore Jr Bridge) offers an easier take out. Take out is after the bridge before the dam on the river left side. The path for take out is obvious and goes to the road for the parking area. Take out before the dam, as this dam can be dangerous.

Directions to Put In

Out of the parking lot, turn right (west) for 0.1 miles to the stop sign.
At stop sign, turn left (south) onto Florence Rd.
Take Florence Rd for 1 mile to Broad St(Hwy 41) traffic light.
Turn left (southeast) onto Broad (Hwy 41).
Take Hwy 41 for 4 miles to traffic light for Hwy 268.
Turn (north) left onto Hwy 268 (Thompson Lane).
Take Thompson Lane for 0.6 miles to the Thompson Lane Greenway Trailhead.
Turn right into the Greenway. In the left corner of the parking area is a canoe access area.

Put In Access

The canoe access put in is very convenient. It is a cement pad right next to the river at the end of a drop off lane called the canoe access road.

Interesting Points Along the Trip

Right after the put in is a Civil War Monument and Park. It is actually worth checking out before or after the paddle. At the beginning of this trip, there are a number of houses for viewing from the river. This section has a number of drops and riffles, adding to the interest of the run. One drop to watch for is the dam after the Murfreesboro sewage treatment plant, which dumps water into the West Fork. This dam has a chute in the center, and it's fun to run through.

28

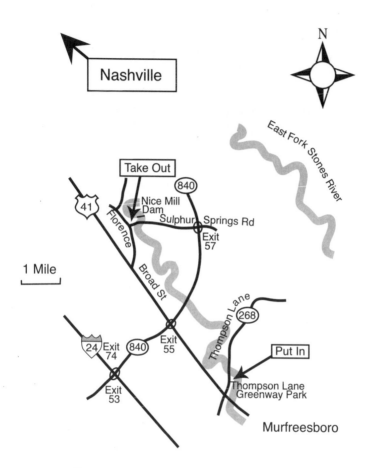

Stones River West Fork

Thompson Lane Greenway to Nice Dam Site

Paddle #8

Precautions

Watch for the break in the dam by the treatment plant, running the chute carefully in the middle of the broken dam. This plant is shortly after a bridge about 2.5 miles from put in. At the end of the trip, avoid going over the Nice Mill Dam as the break in that dam has numerous rocks scattered around, some with metal bars sticking out, which have the potential to be dangerous. As always watch for strainers, deadfalls and the rocky ledges.

Total Length

This trip is 6.7 miles, which can take 3 to 4 hours to paddle depending on stops and flow.

Season

Water levels are generally suitable for running all year long.

Map of the River

TN Atlas Map 38

Picnic spot above Nice Mill Dam

Stones River West Fork

Paddle #9 Nice Mill Dam Site
To the West Fork Boat Ramp

The West Fork of the Stones River is beautiful and quite manageable. There are a number of riffles in the first mile before the water flow slows down. Once the impoundment begins, you are paddling without the aid of any current. The banks of the river are tree lined with the occasional rocky bluff. Except for two littered areas that looked like fishing banks, the float is pristine. There are a number of swimming spots near the rocky ledges and the gentle banks. There are also numerous fishing spots along the route.

Directions to Take Out

From Nashville, head south on Interstate 65 to Exit 59 for 840 East.

Or go east on Interstate 24 to Exit 74B for 840 East toward Knoxville.

Take 840 east to Exit 57 for Sulphur Spring Rd.

At the exit turn left (west) on Sulphur Springs Rd.

Take Sulphur Springs Rd. At 1.7 miles you will pass the Nice Mill Dam Parking lot. (This is the Put In.)

At 1.9 miles,there is a stop sign for Florence Rd.

Turn right onto Florence Rd.

Go another 0.1 miles to next stop sign and again turn right onto Florence Rd.

From this point, continue north on Florence Rd for 3.6 miles to the paved entrance for the West Fork Boat Ramp Rd and parking lot.

Take a sharp right into the entrance road and continue for 0.5 miles.

Parking is available here.

Take Out Access

There is a convenient access area with a ramp into the water and adjacent parking lot compliments of the Army Corps of Engineers and the Percy Priest Dam Project. It is easily spotted as one comes down the river to take out.

Directions to Put In

Proceed down the Ramp Exit Rd to Florence Rd.
Take a left (south) on Florence Rd and continue for 3.6 miles.
At stop sign, turn left (still on Florence) for 0.1 miles.
Turn left onto Sulphur Springs Rd.
Take Sulphur Springs Rd 0.2 miles (over the Al Gore Jr Bridge).
Turn left into the Nice Mill Dam Parking lot.

Put In Access

There is parking on both sides of the dam, but the one south of the dam has better boat access for heading north to the West Fork take out. You want to put in below the dam and avoid going over it. The parking area on the north side of the dam might be better for a picnic as it has shade trees and clearings.

Interesting Points Along the Trip

There are a number of amusing channels and riffles in the first mile. Then it is remarkable to see the effects of the impoundment of the Stones River, with the water flow slowing and the levels deepening. Watch for places along the tree lined banks to picnic, swim or fish.

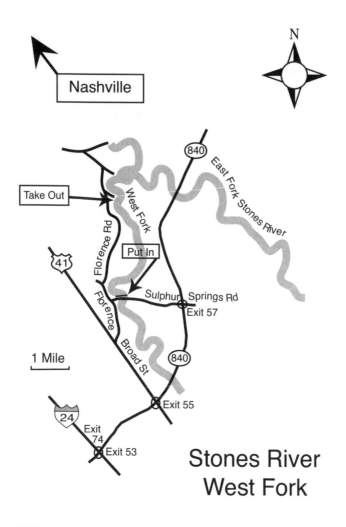

Nashville

Take Out

West Fork

Florence Rd

Put In

Florence

Broad St

840

East Fork Stones River

Sulphur Springs Rd
Exit 57

1 Mile

24

Exit 74

Exit 53

Exit 55

840

41

Stones River
West Fork

Nice Mill Dam to West Fork Boat Ramp

Paddle #9

Precaution

Watch for strainers, deadfalls, and once in the deeper channels, motorboats.

Total Length

The total length of the trip is 5.2 miles, which can take 2.5 to 3 hours.

Season

Water levels are generally suitable for running all year.

Map

TN Atlas Map 38

Nice Mill Dam

Stones River East Fork

Paddle #10 Trimble Rd to Guy James Rd

Trimble Rd to Guy James Rd is a beautiful section of the Stones River as it meanders along farmland and forests with the bluffs of stone that are representative of Middle Tennessee. The water is particularly clear and pools of blue for swimming occur frequently along the way. The area is also known for fishing.

Directions to Take Out

From Nashville, take Interstate 65 South to exit 59 for 840 East.

Or take Interstate 24 East to exit 74 B for 840 East toward Knoxville.

Proceed on 840 to Exit 61 for Rt 266 (Jefferson Pike).

At exit, go right (east). The sign will say Rt 266 north.

Stay on Rt 266 (Jefferson Pike) for 9.5 miles (after the intersection of Rt 231, at 4.4 miles, Rt 266 is identified as Rt 266 East).

At 9.5 miles, there is a stop sign just before the intersection with Rt 96.

At stop sign, bear left for 0.1 miles to stop sign for Rt 96.

At Rt 96, turn right (west).

On Rt 96, continue for 0.2 miles to Browns Mill Rd (just past the gas station).

Turn left (south) onto Browns Mill Rd.

Proceed on Browns Mill Rd for 3.1 miles to Guy James Rd.

At Guy James Rd, turn right (south).

Proceed on Guy James Rd for 0.8 mile. You will see a gravel road along the side of the river (you can park here or 0.2 mile further up on the Guy James Rd by the bridge).

Take out Access

The gravel road joins a number of gravel paths along the river, which appear well used by dirt bikers. The gravel paths go down to the water, allowing easy take out and a short carry or drive, depending where you leave your vehicle.

Directions to Put In

Head back out Guy James Rd (0.8miles –1 mile) to Browns
    Mill Rd.
At Browns Mill Rd, turn right (south east).
Proceed on Browns Mill Rd for 2.1 miles.
Brown Mill Rd ends here at Trimble Rd.
Take a right (south) turn onto Trimble Rd.
Proceed for 0.2 mile to the bridge over the Stones River.

Put In Access

There is a path down to the water on the northwest corner of the bridge. It's easy to guide the boats down the hill here. If the water is particularly low, you may want to take the boats under the bridge for an easy put in on the southwest side of the bridge.   Parking is available along side the road here, or you may want to check with a local landowner about parking on their property to be off the road.

Interesting Points Along the Trip

This is a beautiful run through rural Tennessee farmland and woodland. The meanderings of the river access beauty at every turn. Plenty of wildflowers adorn the banks as well as the limestone rock bluffs of the Cumberland Valley.

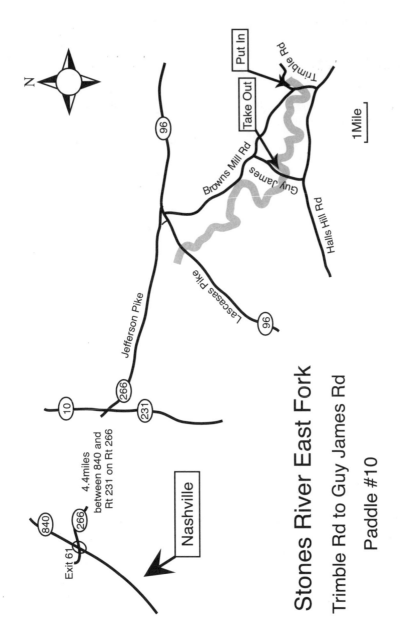

Stones River East Fork

Trimble Rd to Guy James Rd

Paddle #10

Precautions

Deadfalls and the occasional ripple are to be watched for.

Total Length

The trip is 3.5 miles, which can take 2 to 3 hours, depending on stops.

Season

This section can often be run all year, but in dry times when the water is low, the occasional pull over gravel river bottom is necessary.

Map of River

TN Atlas Map 38

Abandoned cars along the river

Stones River East Fork
Paddle #11 Walter Hill Dam to Mona Boat Ramp Landing

The Walter Hill Dam to the Mona Boat Landing section of the Stones River below the Walter Hill Dam, is free flowing for a few miles before slowing down as the river widens into the backwater of the Percy Priest dam. There are a number of fishing spots along this route so you do run into a number of fishermen. Closer to Mona Boat Ramp the water is deep enough to support motorboats so you will want to keep an eye out for them. The rock formations and natural beauty of the river make this a pleasant and easy paddle.

Directions to Take Out

From Nashville, take Interstate 65 South to exit 59 for 840 East. Or take Interstate 24 East to exit 74 B for 840 East.
Proceed on 840 to Exit 61 for Rt 266 (Jefferson Pike).
At the exit, turn right (east). The sign will say Rt 266 north.
Continue on Rt 266 for 1.5 miles.
Turn right onto the Mona Boat Ramp (US Army Corps of Engineer- J Percy Priest Lake).
Follow this road 0.5 miles to the ramp.

Take Out Access

A cement boat ramp makes this an easy and convenient take out. It is easily recognizable from the river at the end of the float. The parking lot here has numerous parking spots for leaving the take out car.

Directions to Put In

Proceed back out the Mona Boat Ramp Rd to Rt 266.

Turn right (east) on to Rt 266.
Proceed on Rt 266 (Jefferson Pike) for 2.7 miles to Rt 231.
Turn right (south) on Rt 231.
In 0.6 miles, Rt 231 crosses the Stones River.
After crossing the bridge, turn left into the park.

Put in Access

The public property at the Walter Hill Dam offers a nice setting for a picnic, swimming, fishing or, best yet, putting in a boat for a paddle on the East Fork of the Stones River. It's an easy portage from the parking lot to the sandbars for put in below the dam.

Interesting Points Along the Trip

This trip has the contrasts of free flowing water below the Walter Hill Dam and the slower water as one approaches the Percy Priest Recreation Center. With the deep, slow water by the Mona Ramp, one has to stay tuned to the possible motorboats and their wake. Between the two public spots of put in and take out, there is plenty of rural Tennessee to enjoy.

Precautions There are deadfalls and motorboats.

Total Length The trip is 5.5 miles which takes about 3 hours to paddle.

Season

This section of the Stones River is open and can be paddled all year.

Map of River TN Atlas Map 38

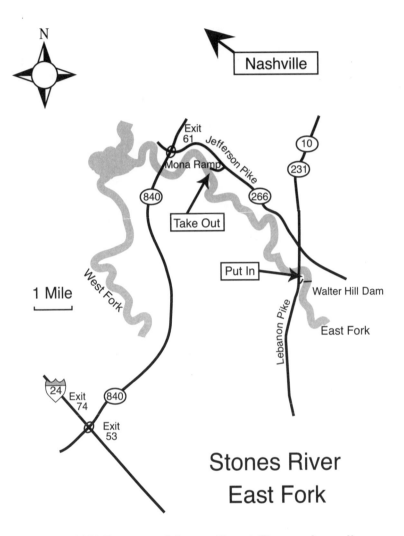

Nashville

N

Exit 61

Jefferson Pike

10

231

Mona Ramp

840

266

Take Out

West Fork

1 Mile

Put In

Walter Hill Dam

Lebanon Pike

East Fork

24

Exit 74

840

Exit 53

Stones River East Fork

Walter Hill Dam to Mona Boat Ramp Landing

Paddle #11

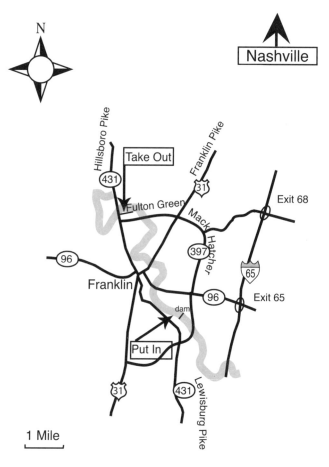

Harpeth River

Lewisburg Pike to the Williamson County
Parks Complex on Fulton Green Lane

Paddle # 12

Harpeth River

The Harpeth River is well known in Middle Tennessee as it flows through Rutherford, Williamson, Davidson, Cheatham, and Dickson counties. Most people are familiar with the Narrows of the Harpeth and paddling there. This river though has a lot more to offer. It has about 117 miles that are good for paddling. In its watershed area, there are numerous creeks that feed into it and also provide good paddling adventures. The six major tributaries of the Harpeth are the West Harpeth, Little Harpeth, South Harpeth, Brush Creek, Turnbull Creek and Jones Creek.

Paddle #12 Franklin Section- Lewisburg Pike to the Williamson County Franklin Parks and Recreation Complex

The 4.7 mile Franklin section of the Harpeth is a very accessible trip for those in Williamson County. The put in and take out are only 3 miles apart. However, there are some downsides too. For part of the trip, the river runs alongside Rt 431 so the road, while it can't be seen above the riverbank, it can be heard. In this section the cars seem louder than the birds. Two other downsides are the visible erosion caused by poor construction practices and the trash along the banks as one goes through town. This said, there are still some interesting rock formations and numerous birds. It's hard not to find beauty along the river but this section makes one aware of the need to protect our rivers.

Directions to Take Out

From Nashville, head south on Hillsboro Rd (Hwy 431). Set your odometer at the intersection of Hillsboro Rd and Old Hickory Blvd.

43

Continue south on Hillsboro Rd for 7.5 miles to Fulton
  Green Rd (traffic light here).
Turn left (east) onto Fulton Green Rd.
Proceed for 0.2 mile to the Williamson County Recreation
  Center in Franklin.
Canoe access road is a gravel road on the left.
Park the car in the Williamson County Recreation Center
  parking lot.

Take Out Access

Check out the look of the river here to be sure you will
recognize it from the river at the end of your paddle. The
bank is fairly steep, but steps and a ladder system for getting boats up and down are here to facilitate the take out. In
wet weather, there may be some added laughs and challenges on the steep muddy bank.

Directions to Put In

Go back on Fulton Green Rd to Hillsboro Rd (Hwy 431).
Turn left (south) on Hillsboro Rd (Business 431).
Continue on Business 431 through the town of Franklin.
431 changes its name to Fifth Ave in Franklin and then
  becomes Lewisburg Pike.
At 3.2 miles (total distance on Hwy 431), turn left onto
  gravel road across from Franklin Country Club.
There are some parking spots here beside the river.

Put In Access

The bank is steep here, but there is a step system set up
to facilitate getting one's boat down to the river. Be sure to
put in downstream from the dam, which can be seen from
this spot.

Interesting Points Along the Trip

Since the banks of the Harpeth are fairly steep in this section, one does get to commune with nature despite the nearness of civilization. At times man's damage to the environment is evident, but fortunately there is a group nearby the Harpeth River Watershed Association that is working to protect and restore the Harpeth. They are located in Franklin and always interested in finding volunteers to work on their restoration projects.

Precautions

The Harpeth is generally wide and slow moving but be cautious following rains. There are always strainers and deadfalls. On this run, be sure to put in downstream of the dam.

Total Length

This 4.7 mile stretch can take 2 to 3 hours depending on flow and stops.

Resource Numbers

The Harpeth River Watershed Association - 615 790 9767.

Season

The Harpeth here can generally be run all year.

Map of the River

TN Atlas Map 37

Harpeth River

Paddle #13 Del Rio Pike to Old Natchez Trace

The Del Rio Pike 7.2 mile segment of the Harpeth makes for an enjoyable outing. There are a number of riffles in the river here, which adds a bit of excitement for the beginner. There are also a number of historical points of interest along this section of the river.

Directions to Take Out

From Nashville, head south on Hillsboro Rd.
At the intersection of Hillsboro Rd and Old Hickory Blvd, set
    your odometer.
Continue south from here for 2.6 miles to Moran Rd.
Turn right (west) at Moran Rd.
Proceed on Moran Rd for 2.4 miles where Moran Rd ends.
Turn left (south) at end of Moran Rd onto the Old Natchez
    Trace (no sign here).
Go a short 0.3 of a mile on Old Natchez Trace to parking
    spots on the left.

Take Out Access

There is a nice path to the water here. Note the surrounding area as you don't want to miss the take out. The next road access is 3 miles down stream. Generally, you can see your parked car from the river here.

Directions to Put In

Continue south on Old Natchez Trace for 2.6 miles ending
    on State 46 Old Hillsboro Rd.
Turn right (south west) onto State 46 (Old Hillsboro Rd).

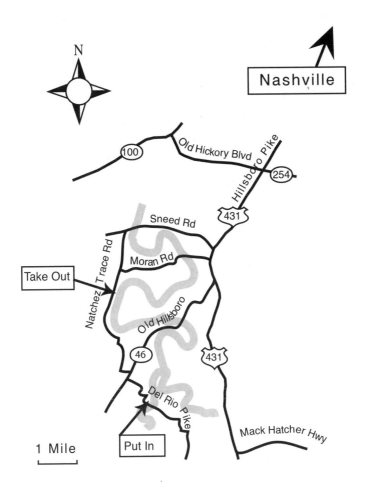

Harpeth River

Del Rio Pike to Old Natchez Trace

Paddle #13

Proceed for a short 0.1 of a mile.

Turn left (south east) onto Del Rio Pike.

Take Del Rio Pike for 1 mile (over the bridge at 0.8mile) to
bridge crossing the river.

Put In Access

There are some parking spots near the bridge; however,
some of the land is posted so get permission if you want to
park on that land. There is a clear path going to the river on
the north side of the bridge.

Interesting Points Along the Trip

Shortly after putting in on this West Fork of the Harpeth,
it joins the Big Harpeth at a place known as the Meeting of
the Waters. This confluence of the rivers marks the site of
the Perkins Family home built in the early 1800's by Thomas
Harden Perkins, Revolutionary War officer and Tennessee
pioneer, planter and ironmaster. Further along the trip as
you paddle along side the Old Natchez Trace, you pass
along Old Town, a highly developed Indian Town now
marked by several earth mounds. You will also see the
remains (dry laid stone abutments) of a bridge built by the
U.S. Government over Brown Creek in 1801 to facilitate
travel on the Natchez Trace.

Precautions

Watch out for occasional deadfalls and riffles.

Total Length

Distance on this trip is 7.2 miles, which can take 3 to 4
hours.

Season

All year

Map of River

TN Atlas Map 37

Where's Waldo?
Be sure to look carefully for the wildlife along the river banks.

.

Harpeth River

Paddle #14
Old Natchez Trace Rd to Moran Rd

The Old Natchez Rd stretch of the Harpeth, just south of Nashville, is ideal for a quick paddle. The length is 3.3 river miles, which depending on intent and river speed, can be a meandering outing or a quick workout. The banks of the Harpeth provide a nice tree canopy for shade. Sandbars are available for the occasional dunking in hot weather. There are only a few riffles and it is wide enough that the few deadfalls are easy to manage so it's a good one for kids or beginners.

Directions to Take Out

From Nashville, head south on Hillsboro Rd.
Set the speedometer at the intersection of Hillsboro Rd and Old Hickory Rd.
Continue on Hillsboro Rd past Old Hickory for 2.6 miles to Moran Rd.
Turn right on Moran Rd.
Proceed on Moran Rd for 0.5 miles to the bridge over the Harpeth River.
Informal parking is available just past the bridge.

Take Out Access

Walk down the path on the southwest corner of the bridge. It is helpful to note a take out plan here as deadfalls may affect where exactly you want to get the boats out. It's a short, manageable incline from the water to the parking areas.

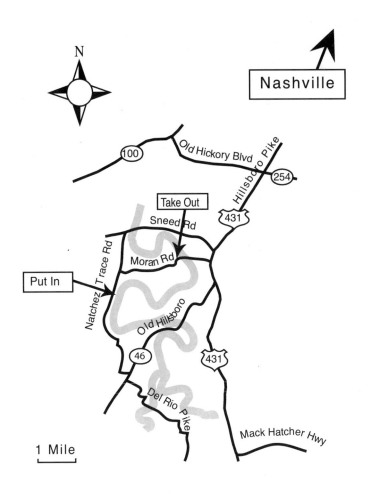

Harpeth River

Old Natchez Trace to Moran Rd

Paddle #14

Directions to Put In

Continue west on Moran Rd. for 1.8 miles until it ends.
Turn left onto Old Natchez Trace (may not be a street sign).
Proceed for 0.3 miles to parking spots along the Harpeth
   River.

Put in Access

There is a nice path with a gentle descent right to the
water from the parking spots.

Interesting Points Along the Trip

After putting in along the Old Natchez Trace Road, the
river quickly heads to the quiet of nature. A number of
estates can be seen from the river including the
Motheral/Moran House built in 1815 by the Revolutionary
War soldier John Motheral. This home is on your right just
before the take out.

Precautions

An occasional deadfall is present, but usually these are
easy to maneuver around, as the river is wide and generally
slow. Note that following strong storms, the placid Harpeth
can rage.

Total Length

The distance of this trip is 3.3 miles, which takes about an
hour to an hour and a half.

Season

This trip can generally be navigated all year, but it is faster when water is running high. In very dry summers, some dragging may be necessary.

Map of River

TN Atlas Map 53

There are a few gentle riffles in this stretch of the Harpeth.

Harpeth River

Paddle #15 Old Natchez Trace Rd to Hwy 100 Canoe Access Area

This Old Natchez Trace to Hwy 100 section of the Harpeth is convenient, close to Nashville and easily accessible. Besides these features, it is beautiful and minimally used. The river runs through farmland, between rolling hillsides and along moss-covered ledges and vine covered woodlands. It provides a tranquil and quiet paddle on a hot summer day.

Directions to Take Out

From Nashville, head south on Hwy 100.
Go past Percy and Edwin Warner Parks.
At the south end of Edwin Warner Park, set your
    odometer.
Go 0.9 miles, just over the green bridge, which
    crosses the Harpeth.
Turn left (east) into the Harpeth Scenic River
    Canoe Access.
Parking spots here are marked and part of the Tennessee
    State Park System.
Daily parking rate is $3 day or $30 for yearly pass
    to all Tennessee State Park access fee areas.
This area is open 7 a.m. until dusk.

Take out Access

It's a good idea to check out the take out while here. The river level will determine where you might want to get out. The green on the bridge is impossible to miss so there is no danger of confusing bridges and getting out at the wrong one. The incline from the water to the paved parking

Harpeth River

Old Natchez Trace to Hwy 100 Canoe Access

Paddle #15

area is easy to manage.

Directions to Put In

Go out the parking lot turning right (northeast) on to
　　Hwy 100.
Take Hwy 100 for 1.5 miles to Old Hickory Blvd (east).
Turn right (east) on Old Hickory Blvd.
Stay on Old Hickory for 2.7 miles to Hillsboro Rd.
Turn right (south) on Hillsboro Rd.
Take Hillsboro Rd for 2.6 miles to Moran Rd.
Turn right (west) onto Moran Rd.
Take Moran Rd (going over the Harpeth river at 0.6miles) for
　　2.5 miles.
Moran Rd ends on Old Natchez Trace Rd.
Turn left (south) onto Old Natchez Trace Rd.
Proceed on Old Natchez Trace Rd for 0.3 miles to parking
　　along the Harpeth.

Put In Access

　　There is a nice short path going from the road to a
shallow water spot for put in. This area can be popular for
swims after school on hot days. There is a nearby rope
swing.

Interesting Points Along the Trip

　　The river here runs through rural and lightly developed
land. The occasional house does not detract from the natural beauty of the Harpeth shores. The woodlands along the
banks make wonderful homes for an abundance of wildlife.
The birds are plentiful and full of songs.

Precautions

Look out for deadfalls and strainers even though the river is wide through this section. On one trip, we had trouble with deadfalls at the Sneed Rd Bridge. It was necessary for us to get out and portage around the bridge. Always be alert to changing conditions. For safety, get out and scout when a questionable situation arises.

Total length

This stretch is 9.5 miles, which can take 4 or 5 hours.

Variations

For a shorter trip you can put in or take out by the bridge going over the Harpeth on Moran Rd. This bridge is 3.3 miles along on this river trip. See previous paddle trip #14.

Season

This section can be paddled all year long.

Map

TN Atlas Map 53

The rope swing: do I dare?

Harpeth River

Paddle #16 Hwy 100 to Newsome Station Mill

The Hwy 100 to Newsome Station Mill run along the Harpeth is easy and very convenient. The length offers some challenge and a good work out. Both put in and take out are facilitated by the State Access Parking Pay System. This means there is a paved area to leave you car and a $3 fee for doing so. (Year long access pass to all State Parks is $30.) This run is entirely in Davidson county, so it is convenient to Nashville. The tree lined banks make this run feel more remote than it actually is. In the course of the run, the river loops under the railroad bridge three times, under power lines and under Interstate 40 once, but these intrusions on the float only serve to make the rest of the trip seem more serene.

Directions to Take Out

From Nashville, head west on Interstate 40.
Take Interstate 40 to Exit 192 for Pegram (McCrory Lane).
Go right (north) off the exit ramp onto McCrory Lane.
Stay on McCrory Lane for 0.1 miles to Newsome Station Rd
   (traffic light here).
Go right (east) on Newsome Station Rd.
Take Newsome Station for 1.9 miles until it ends (after going
   through a bridge underpass).
Turn right onto Dead End road and go 0.1 miles to the
   entrance for the Newsome Station Mill Park (on left).

Take Out Access

A paved fee parking lot is above the mill dam and the take out is obvious. The remnants of the dam are just visible on the far sides. The bank formed by the left remnant of

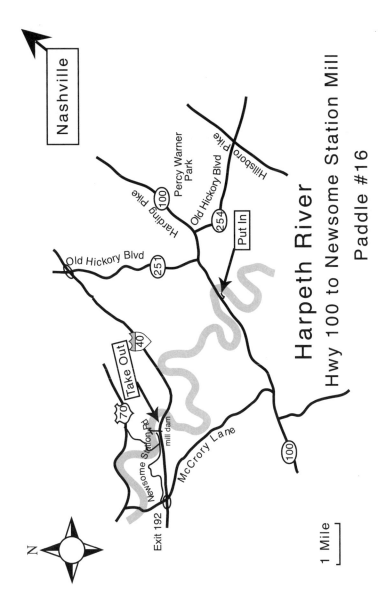

Harpeth River
Hwy 100 to Newsome Station Mill
Paddle #16

the dam makes take out on river left easy.

Directions to Put In

Go right, out the parking lot to stop sign.
Turn left under the bridge onto Newsome Station Rd.
Continue on Newsome Station Rd for 1.9 miles to McCrory
    Lane.
Turn left (south) on McCrory Lane.
Take McCrory Lane for 4.4 miles to Hwy 100.
Turn left (northeast) onto Hwy 100.
Take Hwy 100 for 2.8 miles to Harpeth River Access Area
    on right.
Turn right here (prior to green bridge that crosses the
    Harpeth River).

Put In Access

From the paved fee parking area, there is a gentle down-
hill path that goes under the bridge and offers convenient
access.

Interesting Points Along the Trip

The undersides of the Interstate and the railroad bridges
are interesting from an engineering point of view. For the
most part, this is a gentle run with a few riffles along tree
lined banks. When the foliage is out, you cannot see all the
activity that must be near. There are plenty of birds, wildflowers and wildlife. The occasional cow is also to be found
cooling off as you paddle along. The remains of the
Newsome Station Mill are at the take out and are worth
exploring. This is a State Park where restoration work is
keeping the history of the Newsome Station Mill site alive.

Precautions

Watch for strainers and deadfalls. Also check water levels after heavy rains, as the Harpeth can flood.

Total Length

The length of this trip is 9.5 miles, which can take from 4 to 5 hours depending on flow and stops.

Season

Water levels are suitable for paddling all year long.

Map of the River

TN Atlas Map 52

The remains of the Newsome Station Mill along the Harpeth.

Harpeth River

Paddle #17 Bridge Route 249 to Bridge on Route 70 and Cedar Hill Road

This route is a beautiful quiet section of the Harpeth, making two westerly loops as the river heads north between Pegram and Kingston Springs in Cheatham county. There are a number of riffles and minimal intrusions by man. A number of streams join the Harpeth here, some with waterfalls adding their own natural beauty to the cruise.

Directions to Take Out

From Nashville, head west on Interstate 40 to Exit 192 for Pegram.
At the exit, turn right (north) toward Pegram on McCrory Lane.
Stay on McCrory Lane for 1.2 to where it ends on Hwy 70.
Turn left (west) on Hwy 70.
Take Hwy 70 for 5.4 miles to Cedar Hill Rd (before bridge over the Harpeth).
Turn right (north) onto Cedar Hill Rd.
Immediately after getting on Cedar Hill Rd, pull into the parking area on left.

Take Out Access

From the parking lot, head down the gravel and dirt road to familiarize yourself with the take out. You'll notice a sign prior to the bridge indicating the Foggy Bottom canoe take out. Before reaching the bridge, the take out has stone steps and is more gradual than the take out after the bridge.

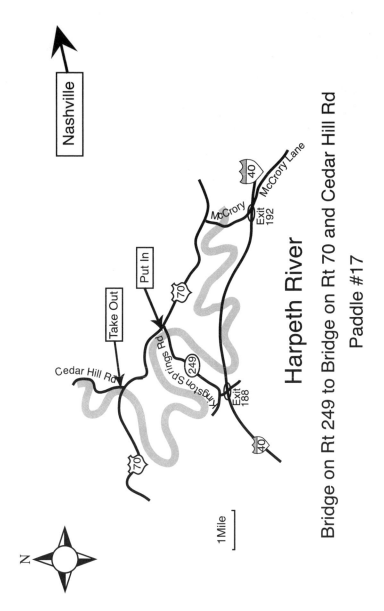

Harpeth River

Bridge on Rt 249 to Bridge on Rt 70 and Cedar Hill Rd

Paddle #17

Directions to Put In

Go out the parking lot and turn right (south) onto
    Cedar Hill Rd.
Immediately turn left (east) onto Hwy 70.
Stay on Hwy 70 for 2.2 miles to Rt 249.
Turn right (south) onto Rt 249.
On Rt 249, cross over railroad track and pull into the gravel
    parking area just before the bridge over the Harpeth
    River.

Put In Access

Follow the dirt and gravel path down to the bridge for an
easy access to the Harpeth River.

Interesting Points Along the Trip

This route goes by the Kingston Springs City Park with
23 acres next to the river. There is a canoe ramp here so if
you want to get out and look around it's easy. There is an
old railroad bridge that is supported by pilings built during
the Civil War here, as well as picnic areas with grills if that
interests you. As you do this paddle, keep alert to streams
that join the Harpeth. One such stream joining the river
from the left has a little waterfall about 20 feet upstream in a
wooded cove.

Precautions

Deadfall and strainers are along the way, but the river is so
wide that they generally don't provide much of a problem.
This is a good run for beginners.

Total Length

This trip is 8.4 miles long, which can take 4 to 5 hours.

Variations

The Kingston Springs City Park is 4 miles into this 8.4 mile trip and can be used as a put in or take out for a shorter trip.

Resource Numbers

Adventure Harpeth Tip-A-Canoe: 615-646-7124
Foggy Bottom: 615-952-4062
Canoe Music City: 615-952-4211

Season This section can be paddled all year

Map TN Atlas Map 52

Waterfalls on a creek joining the Harpeth. Paddle up to this from the Harpeth for a good picture opportunity in front of the falls. Note: this route does not go over the falls!

Harpeth River

Paddle #18 Narrows of the Harpeth

This 5 mile stretch of river is well known in Nashville and offers a number of features for paddlers. Because the river makes a big loop, the put in is barely 400 yards from the take out. Yet by water, the route is a little over 5 miles of beautiful river. This feature allows for an easy one car put in and take out.

The put in for this trip is close to the hole Montgomery Bell drilled through 290 feet of limestone ridge located at the Narrows. This engineering feat was accomplished around 1818. The resulting opening in the limestone provided rushing water to be used as a power source for his iron manufacturing operation. It is worth the few minutes it takes to go down the wooden walkway to see the work done by Montgomery Bell and slaves. This site is a National Historic Landmark, as well as a National Historic Engineering Landmark. One can also walk up the short trail to view the Narrows from above the tunnel. This spot offers a beautiful vista of the river on both sides of the Narrows. Note: it is too dangerous to ride through the tunnel.

Montgomery Bell's Tunnel the Narrows of the Harpeth

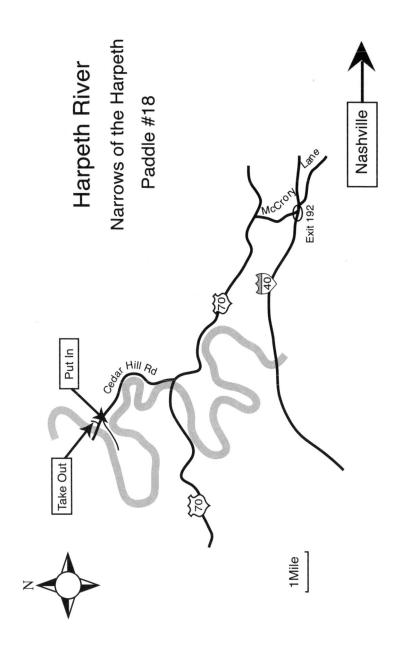

Harpeth River
Narrows of the Harpeth
Paddle #18

Nashville

McCrory Lane

Exit 192

40

70

70

Put In

Cedar Hill Rd

Take Out

N

1 Mile

The fast water, deadfalls, boulders, debris and variable space for head clearance make going through this tunnel extremely dangerous.

A number of outfitters offer canoe rentals, with assistance in transporting for put in and take out. State park land is available for parking at both put in and take out. The put in offers a few trails for hiking, and the take out has a number of picnic tables in a park setting. The take out is also a fun place to swim with a moderate current running along the pebble flat sandbar.

The attractiveness of the Narrows means that unless you are paddling during the week or in questionable weather, you are bound to be sharing this part of nature with a number of others.

Directions to Put In

From Nashville, head west on Interstate 40 to Exit 192 for Pegram.
At the exit, turn right (north) to Pegram on McCrory Lane.
Stay on McCrory Lane for 1.2 miles until it ends on Hwy 70.
Turn left (west) on Hwy 70.
Take Hwy 70 for 5.4 miles to Cedar Hill Rd (before bridge over Harpeth River).
Turn right (north) onto Cedar Hill Rd.
Take Cedar Hill Rd for 2.8 miles.
Turn left into Narrows of the Harpeth State Park.
Follow Park road for 0.4 miles to Canoe Ramp and parking spots

Put in Access

A great ramp and stairs adjacent to the parking area make getting down this steep bank quite manageable. This is a TN State Park so you will have the option of paying a daily parking fee of $3 or buying an annual pass for $30.

Directions to Take Out

After unloading your boat, go back to Cedar Hill Rd.
Turn left (or west) onto Cedar Hill Road and just across the
street prior to the Harris Street Bridge is the State Park Boat
Access Area. Now the car will be waiting for you at the end
of your paddle. You just have to walk back across the street
to the put in and your waiting boat.

Take out access

Once you pass under the Harris Street Bridge, pull up on
the pebble sand bar on the right. Here you have the choice
of bringing the car down for easy loading or carrying the
boat up the path to the parking lot.

Interesting Points Along the Trip

The entrance to Montgomery Bell's tunnel can be seen
from the river on the right shortly after getting in the water.
To view the other side of this tunnel, watch for a stream that
joins the Harpeth on the river to the right about 5 miles
along the trip or about a half mile before the bridge. Paddle
upstream a short distance to see this historic site and scenic waterfall. Park your boat and look around at old iron
scraps and look for Montgomery's gravesite.

Precautions

Watch for deadfalls and strainers. In bends of the river,
they seem to call out to overturn canoes. Following very
heavy rains and flood stage flows, the rental companies will
close, as paddling isn't safe at these times.

Total length

The total length of the trip is 5.5 miles. It usually takes 3 hours, but add time on for swims or picnicking.

Resource Numbers

Foggy Bottom 615-952-4062 canoe rentals
Music City Canoe 615-952-4211 canoe rentals
Tip-A-Canoe 615-646-7124 canoe rentals

Season

This trip can be made any time of the year.

Map of River

TN Atlas Map 52

Vista above the Narrows

Duck River

The Duck River flows in Middle Tennessee from east to west, eventually joining the Tennessee River where it is known as Kentucky Lake. It is the longest river contained entirely in Tennessee and flows through miles of remotely populated countryside. There are many miles of beautiful paddling available but be aware of the dams and be prepared to portage around them. A large power generating dam built by the TVA is in Normandy creating Normandy Lake. Other dams are the remains of old mills. Be alert for the sight of slack water with the sound of rushing water ahead.

Usually the Duck is a gentle river with a gradual gradient, but it can be swift in times of high water or when the dams upstream are releasing water. We paddled downstream from Normandy Lake a few days prior to an expected hurricane. In anticipation of heavy rains, the TVA had opened the Normandy Dam to minimize the strain of added rainwater on the dam. It is always a good idea to call the TVA water release number (800-238-2264) prior to a paddle downstream from a dam.

Paddle #19 Normandy Dam to Three Bridge Fork Rd

This stretch of the Duck is generally quiet and gentle as it meanders through woodland, farmland and along rocky bluffs. The river is pristine in this sparsely populated area. Wildlife is abundant along the shores, and the wild flowers beautiful in the growing season. Putting in below the Normandy dam, you will want to be aware of the Cortner Mill Dam and be prepared to portage this.

Directions to Take Out

71

From Nashville, head south on Interstate 65.

Take Interstate 65 to Exit 59A for 840 East (Knoxville).

Proceed on 840 for 11 miles to Exit 42 (Shelbyville 31A, 41A).

At Exit 42, turn right (south) on 31A, 41A.

Proceed for 2.6 miles and when 31A and 41A split, bear left on 41A.

Stay on 41A for 33.4 miles through Shelbyville to Normandy Rd. (Normandy Rd is 2.2 miles south of the bridge going over the Duck on 41A.)

Turn left (east) onto Normandy Rd.

Go on Normandy Rd for 0.5 miles to Three Bridge Fork Rd.

Turn left (north) onto Three Bridge Fork Rd for 1.5 miles.

When the road forks with Bill Russell bear left (north).

Continue on Three Bridge Fork Rd for 0.6 mile.

Turn right into the parking lot just before the bridge crosses the Duck River.

Take Out Access

The parking area is gravel and offers broad cement stairs to the Duck River. The stairs are popular for fishing and facilitate an easy exit at this spot. Note the landmarks for the end of your float as the area prior to the Cortner Rd Bridge (along this route) also has stairs prior to a bridge.

Directions to Put In

Leave the parking lot, turning left onto Three Bridge Fork Rd.

At 0.6 miles, bear right continuing on Three Bridge Fork Rd for another 1.5 miles.

At Normandy Rd, turn left (east).

Proceed on Normandy Rd for 4.1 miles to the town of Normandy.

Cross the railroad tracks and turn left onto Front Street.

Continue on Front Street for 1.2 miles to the entrance marker for River Access.

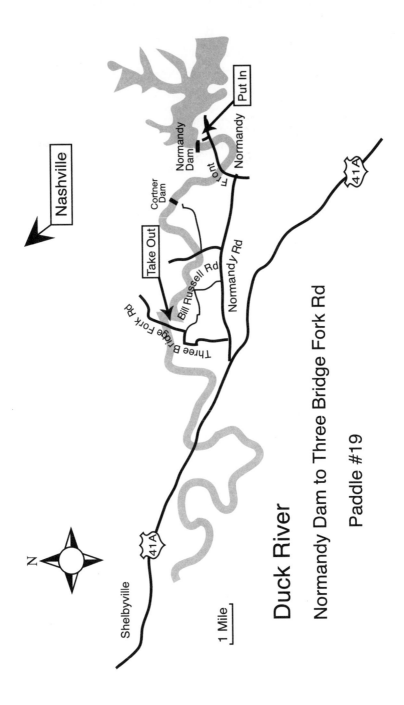

Nashville

Put In

Normandy Dam

Cortner Dam

Normandy

Front

Take Out

Bill Russell Rd

Normandy Rd

Three Bridge Fork Rd

41A

Shelbyville

41A

N

1 Mile

Duck River
Normandy Dam to Three Bridge Fork Rd

Paddle #19

This is right below the Normandy Dam. (You might want to explore the Lake area up here.)
Turn left into the parking area for the Duck River.

Put In Access

There are a number of convenient put in places along this tree lined parking area. Pick a parking spot and make your way to the sidewalk-like entrance into the Duck River.

Interesting Points Along the Trip

About 3.5 miles downstream from the Normandy Dam is the Cortner Mill Dam. This definitely needs to be portaged. Coming down the river, you will note slack water with the sound of rushing water ahead. The mill is on the left of the river. You can take out at the weir on river on the left or portage on the right. There is a restaurant at the mill which serves a brunch on Sunday between 11:30 and 1:30 and dinner Tuesday through Saturday right on the river. They recommend calling ahead just in case there is a private party that day. The take out for exploring or a meal is right below the restaurant/mill/dam on the left. There are parking spots here, if you prefer this spot for a put in or take out.

Precautions

Watch for the Cortner Mill Dam, strainers, deadfalls and high water following heavy rains or a major release of dam water by the TVA.

Total Length

Total length is 8.5 miles, which can take from 3 to 5 hours depending on flow and stops.

Variations

You can put in at the Cortner Mill Restaurant if you prefer to miss the portage around the dam. Another variation is to put in below the Normandy Dam and take out at the cement stairs just prior to the Cortner Rd Bridge. This would be a trip of 5.3 miles.

Resources Numbers

TVA Information Line: 800-238-2264 or 865-632-6065 (for a specific question)
Cortner Mill Restaurant: 931-857-3017 or 800-876-3017

Season

There is plenty of water in this section of the Duck, and it can be paddled all year.

Map

TN Atlas Map 22

Rock skipping along the banks of the river

Duck River

Paddle #19 Rt 99/431 to Carpenter Bridge Road

This gentle and scenic stretch of the Duck River flows between lush tree lined banks in rural Maury County. This section of the Duck is a designated a scenic river. Generally, the water is slow but moving, characteristics of a Class 1 river, so it is ideal for the beginning paddler. The river is also biologically rich so it is popular with fishermen.

Directions to Take Out

From Nashville, head south on Interstate 65.
Continue on 65 S to exit 46 for Rt 99 and Rt 412.
Head east from the exit (NOT west to Columbia).
Take Rt 99 east for 1.3 miles to Carpenter Bridge Rd.
Turn right (south) onto Carpenter Bridge Rd.
Follow Carpenter Bridge Rd for 1.7 mile to gravel road right
    before the bridge.
Turn right onto gravel road and parking lot.

Take Out Access

This public access and parking area is part of the Duck River Wildlife Management Area. Parking is available in a gravel lot, and there is a very convenient, gentle-grade, wide path to the water. When paddling, take out is just beyond the Carpenter Bridge, which has the remains of a steel bridge structure next to it, so it is easy to identify.

Directions to Put In

Head back out the gravel parking area.
Turn left (north) onto Carpenter Bridge Rd.

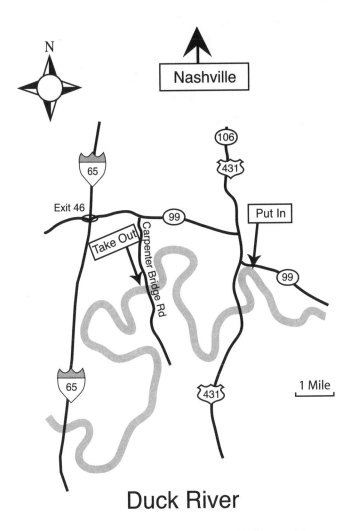

Duck River

Rt 99/431 to Carpenter Bridge Rd

Paddle #20

On Carpenter Bridge Rd for 1.7 miles to intersection with
Rt 99.

Turn right (east) on Rt 99.

Follow Rt 99 east for 2.8 miles to the intersection with
Rt 431.

At Rt 431, turn right (south) for less than a mile where
Rt 431junctions with Rt 99 east again.

At this junction of Rt 99 east and Rt 431 turn left (east) and
note River Rats Canoe Rental.

Put In Access

River Rats Canoe Rental allows parking and put in for a
minimal ramp fee. They have a nice gravel road down to
the river, making access ideal and convenient.

Interesting Points Along the Trip

The banks along this section of the scenic Duck are lush
with assorted vegetation including an array of wild flowers
and a variety of hardwoods. Tall bluffs and rocky cliffs are
interspersed along the way.

Precautions

Watch for fallen trees and strainers, but generally, the
river is wide enough to avoid these. However, just past the
first bridge, which goes under Rt 431, are the remnants of
an old dam. Scout out the area. Usually one can keep to
the left and do fine.

Total Distance

This trip is 9 miles and takes about 4 to 5 hours to paddle.

Season

This section of the Duck can be paddled all year.

Resource number

River Rat's Canoe Rental: 931-381-2278

Map

TN Atlas Map 37

Even the dog likes this trip!

Piney River

Paddle #21 Interstate 40 to Piney River Road

Starting in Dickson County and traveling south through Hickman County to the bridge on Piney Road, this 6 mile segment of the Piney is a very pleasant stretch. It has numerous rocky cliffs and beautiful pools of clear blue water. Strainers and deadfalls keep one alert. In addition, be on the lookout for barbed wire fencing strung across the river to keep the cattle from wandering too far from home.

Directions to Take Out

From Nashville, head west on Interstate 40 to Exit 163 Centerville (Rt 48).
At the exit stop sign, turn left (south) onto Rt 48.
Proceed south on Rt 48 for 4.9 miles to Piney River Rd.
Turn left (east) onto Piney River Rd.
Take this road for 0.4 miles to the bridge, which crosses the Piney River.
There are a few parking spots just before the bridge on the northwest side of the bridge.

Take out Access

The the second bridge alerts one to the approach of the take out. Exiting on the river right, just prior to the bridge will put you on the northwest corner of the bridge. From here there is a worn path that will take you to the parking spots above the bank. It is an easy carry up to your waiting car. It's always a good idea to familiarize yourself with the take out scene prior to the trip.

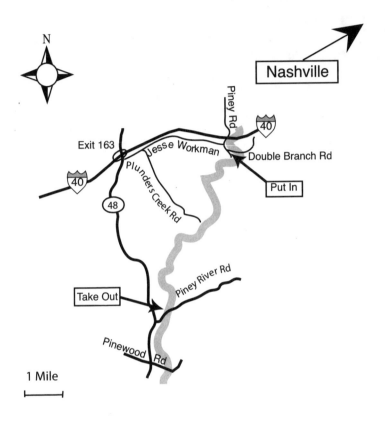

Piney River

Interstate 40 to Piney River Rd

Paddle #21

Directions to Put In

From the bridge on Piney River Rd, go back west for 0.4
miles to Rt 48.
Turn right (north) on Rt 48.
Continue on Rt 48 for 4.8 miles to Plunders Creek Rd.
Plunders Creek Rd is just before (south of) Interstate 40.
Turn right (east) onto Plunders Creek Rd.
Take Plunders Creek Rd for 0.5 miles to Jesse Work Rd.
Bear left onto Jesse Work Rd (which parallels the interstate)
for 2.3 miles.
Jesse Work Rd ends on Piney Rd at the Piney River.
For a better put in, turn right onto Piney Rd.
Go 0.1 miles to the first left onto Double Branch Rd.
Proceed on Double Branch Rd for 0.2 miles to a low water
crossing over the Piney River.
There are a few parking spaces next to the low water
crossing.

Put In Access

The sandbar next to the low water crossing makes an
excellent and easy put in.

Precautions

Watch for deadfalls, strainers and the above-mentioned
barbed wire that one farmer has strung across the river to
keep his cattle from roaming in the river. Along the creek
bed, the wire is easy to lift up and pass the boat under.
Then just climb over, between or under to reconnect with
the boat.

Total Length

Total length of this trip is 6 miles, which can take 3 to 4 hours depending on stops and water flow.

Season

This trip can be done from November until June. As always, water level is weather dependent. The put in has some of the lowest levels of the trip from which you can judge how high the river is running.

Map

TN Atlas 35

Put In next to low water crossing

Piney River

Paddle #22 Piney River Road Bridge to Walter Nunnely Bridge

This beautiful section of the Piney River runs through Hickman county. The beginning of this 6.9 mile cruise starts slowly but quickly picks up in beauty. There are a number of limestone structures along the way. The wildflowers here are outstanding. Birds and wildlife abound. On one trip, we spotted a black goat in a limestone cave high above the river.

Directions to Take Out

From Nashville, head west on Interstate 40 to Exit 163 for Centerville (Rt 48).
At the exit, turn left (south) on Rt 48.
Proceed on Rt 48 for 10.8 miles to the junction of Rt 230 in Nunnelly.
Turn right (west) onto Rt 230.
Continue on Rt 230 for 2.1 miles to an unmarked dirt road just before the bridge.
Be careful leaving the road if you have a low underside to your car.
Parking spaces are available under the Walter Nunnely Bridge.

Take out Access

This take out is a popular swimming spot for locals so you will often have company here. Take out is easiest on the left side of the river just after going under the bridge. There is plenty of flat land to pull up your boat and an easy carry to where you parked your car.

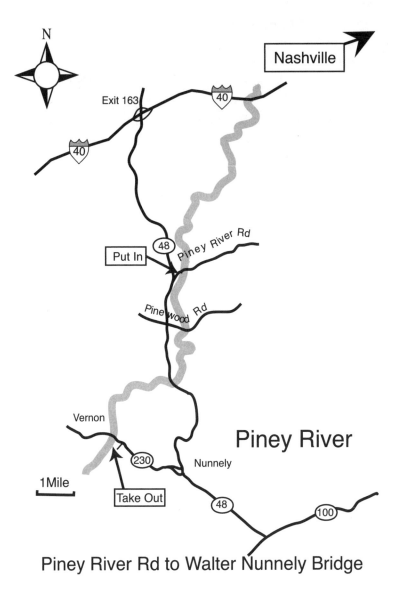

Piney River

Piney River Rd to Walter Nunnely Bridge

Paddle #22

Directions to Put In

Go back up the dirt road to Rt 230.
Turn right (east) onto Rt 230.
Continue on Rt 230 for 2.1 miles to Rt 48.
Turn left (north) onto Rt 48.
Proceed on Rt 48 for 5.9 miles to Piney River Rd.
Turn right (east) onto Piney River Rd.
Go a short 0,4 miles to the bridge over the Piney River.
There are a few spots on the northwest corner of the bridge
    for parking.

Put In Access

A worn tire track path will take you down the hill to the
put in. It's an easy carry/slide with a convenient put in right
before the bridge.

Interesting Points Along the Trip

This is a great paddle through rural Tennessee. The
water is clear with blue swimming holes along the way.
Cattle farms and forests add to the pastoral beauty of this
trip. In addition, some of the most outstanding rock formations are along this stretch of the Piney River.

Precautions

Deadfalls and strainers plague this stream or make it
interesting depending on your point of view. Navigation
skills are necessary. Fun currents abound, keeping one
alert.

Total Length

This trip is 6.9 miles and takes from 3 to 4 hours depending on stops and water flow.

Season

This section can usually be paddled all year. In particularly dry times you may have to drag your boat over shallow areas.

Map

TN Atlas Map 35

One of many rocky cliffs along the Piney River

Piney River

Paddle #23
Brook to Piney River Canoe and Camp

This is a shorter variation of the previous Piney River paddle trip #22. It is a 4.5 mile stretch facilitated by the Piney River Canoe and Camp operation. You can rent canoes and kayaks from them. In addition, if you have your own boat but need a shuttle to put in, they offer that service as well. Their location is a great take out and a convenient spot to leave your car. However, if you want a longer trip, they will shuttle your car to the Nunnely Bridge and you to the put in. It's a beautiful stretch of the Piney as it heads south through Pinewood.

Directions to Take Out

From Nashville, head west on Interstate 40 to
    Exit 163 for Centerville (Rt 48).
At the exit, turn left (south) onto Rt 48.
Proceed on Rt 48 for 6.6 miles to Cash HLW Rd.
Turn right (east) onto Cash HLW Rd.
Take Cash Rd for 1 mile to the Pinewood Canoe
    and Camp location.

Take Out Access

Both the Piney River Canoe and Camp and the Nunnally Bridge are visible from the River. Additionally, they both provide flat stretches to exit from the river and easy carries to your car.

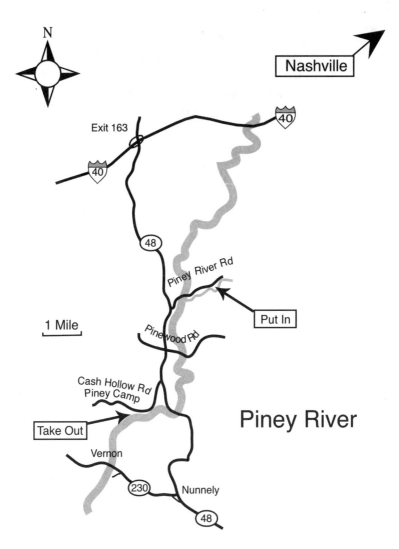

Brook to Piney River Canoe and Camp

Paddle #23

Directions to Put In

The Pinewood Canoe and Camp own land adjacent to a creek, which flows a short distance into the Piney River. They will shuttle you or give directions to this area, which is just beyond the Piney River Road Bridge.

From the Pinewood Canoe and Camp, head back
    on Cash HLW Rd to Rt 48.
Turn left (north) onto Rt 48.
Proceed on Rt 48 for 1.7 miles to the
    Piney River Rd.
Turn right on Piney River Rd.
Go 0.4 miles to the Piney River Rd Bridge.

Private land owned by Pinewood Canoe and Camp is
    a short distance beyond the bridge, with a creek
    flowing into the river.

Diving at the Pinewood Canoe and Camp Area

Interesting points along the trip

Unique rock formations, awesome cliffs and blue water swimming holes are the highlights of this pretty little run. The Pinewood Cattle Company owns some of the land along this part of the Piney so you will see pastoral scenes with cattle. At the Canoe and Camp location, there is a diving board mounted on rock, as well as a rope swing. It is a fun trip.

Precautions

Deadfall and strainers in this narrow river offer a moderate challenge. Navigation skills are needed here.

Rope swing at Pinewood Canoe and Camp

Total Length

The distance for this run is 4.5 miles, which can take 3 to 4 hours. Be sure to allow time to play at the take out.

Resource Numbers

Pinewood Canoe and Camp: 931-729-1042 for rentals and/or shuttles

Season

This section of the Piney can usually be paddled all year. In particularly dry times, you may have to drag your boat over the shallow areas.

Map

TN Atlas 35

A fun family excursion!

Buffalo River

Paddle #24 Near Interstate 40
Seedtick Rd to Cuba Land Rd

The Buffalo River offers more than 100 miles of floating opportunities. It flows west through Lawrence County then turns north near Flatwood as works its way to the Duck River near Kentucky Lake.

This stretch of the Buffalo is beautiful, easily accessible and especially convenient if you only have one transport vehicle. Eddie from the Buffalo River Camping and Canoeing at the take out destination will cart you and your boats to one of two put ins There is a 10.6 miler or a 4.5 miler. He charges a fee for boat for ramp landing at his place if you have your own boat. You can leave your car here and arrange put in transportation. He also has a rental service for canoes and a few kayaks. This place is much busier on sunny summer weekends than in off-season or on the quiet weekdays. Call ahead.

Directions to Take Out

From Nashville, head west on Interstate 40 to
    Exit #143 for Lobelville (Hwy 13).
At exit ramp, turn left (south) toward Lobelville
    onto Hwy 13.
Continue on Hwy 13 for 1 mile to Cuba Landing Rd.
Turn right (west) onto Cuba Landing Rd.
Follow Cuba Landing Rd for 0.7 miles to Buffalo
    River Camping and Canoeing (on your right after   crossing bridge over the Buffalo River).

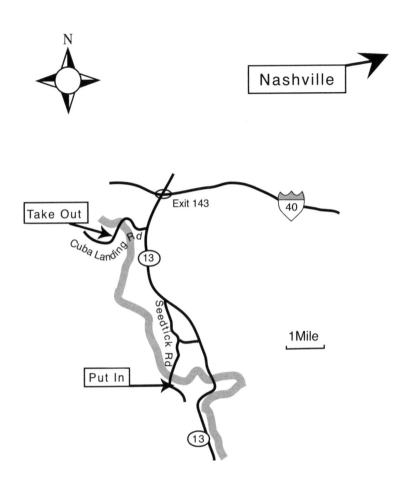

Buffalo River

Seedtick Rd to Cuba Landing Rd

Paddle #24

Take Out Access

Finishing this river cruise, you will see the take out on the left after going under a bridge. This is clearly marked by Eddie. There is a cement ramp for easy take out. Be sure to move boats away as fellow paddlers may be following you and may want to use the same take out spot.

Directions to Put In

From the Canoe and Camping area turn left back
    onto Cuba Landing Rd.
Take Cuba Landing Rd 0.7miles to Hwy 13.
At Hwy 13 turn right (south).
Continue on Hwy 13 for 1.9 miles to Seedtick Rd.
Turn right (west) on Seedtick Rd.
Proceed on Seedtick Rd for 1.2 miles then bear right
    when road splits.
Continue for another 1.2 miles to second bridge,
    which crosses the Buffalo River.
Under this bridge are parking spots and a turn around but
    access appears private. Ask permission.

Put In Access

Put in is an easy carry from parking area down to river.

Variation in Route

The Buffalo Camp and Canoe also has access to a put in off Hwy 13. For a fee, arrangements can be made to put in here for a 10.6 mile trip

Interesting Points Along the Trip

The Buffalo keeps its clear water as it winds its way to the
Duck River. The swimming holes along are beautifully blue
and clear. The rock ledges offer interesting scenery. One
rock formation high above the river is known as Standing
Rock (just beyond Standing Rock Bridge). The river is also
known for fishing and wildlife along its shores.

Precautions

Even though the Buffalo River is wide and generally slow
moving, there are places where the river bends and the current picks up. Deadfalls in these areas can be hazardous.
Be alert, avoiding deadfalls and strainers; also stay to the
inside of turns where possible.

Total Length

This is either a 4.5 mile run or a 10.6 mile run, which can
take 3 to 5 hours depending on trip, stops, and river flow.

Cows along the banks of the Buffalo

Resource number

Buffalo River Camping & Canoeing – 931 296-5964

Season

Generally water levels are suitable for paddling all year long.

Map of the River

TN Atlas Map 35

Rocky cliff high above the Buffalo River

River Trips

Creek Trips

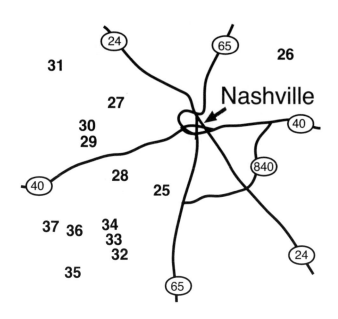

25. West Harpeth - Leipers Fork to Rt 96
26. Bledsoe Creek - Rogana Rd to Old Union Access
27. Sycamore Creek - Water Plant Rd to Rt 12
28. Turnbull Creek - Hwy 96 to Ulrich Landing Park
29. Jones Creek - Jones Creek Rd to Petty Rd
30. Jones Creek - Petty Rd to Timber Ridge Rd
31. Yellow Creek - Rt 13 to Rt 149 Wildlife Refuge
32. Big Swan Creek - Natchez Trace Pky to Horse
    Branch Rd
33. Big Swan Creek - Horse Branch Rd to Releigh
    Chapel Rd
34. Big Swan Creek - Releigh Chapel Rd to Duck River
35. Fortyeight Creek - Fortyeight Creek Rd to Buffalo River
36. Cane Creek - Farmers Exchange to Pleasantville
37. Cane Creek - Hwy 100 to Hwy 438

The creeks here tend to be narrower than the rivers, have faster currents, and are often more remote. They are generally full of deadfalls. This combination requires more precise maneuvering skills to paddle safely.

A quiet section of a tree lined creek

West Harpeth

Paddle #25 Leipers Fork to Hwy 96

This branch of the Harpeth flows northerly from Leipers Fork to the west of Franklin. At the start of the trip, the creek is quite narrow, with high banks. For most of the route, trees provide a shading canopy, which is fortunate as the water is murky and not that inviting for swimming. There are a number of sand bars for a rest or picnic.

Directions to Take Out

Head south from Nashville on Hillsboro Rd (Rt 431).
Start your odometer at the intersection of Old Hickory Rd
     (Rt 254) and Hillsboro Rd
Continue south for 3.2 miles to Old Hillsboro Rd (Rt 46).
Turn right (west) at the light onto Rt 46.
Continue on Old Hillsboro Rd (Rt 46) for 5.6 miles to Rt 96.
At Rt 96 turn left (east).
Proceed for 0.3 of a mile to the bridge over the West
     Harpeth.

Take Out Access

This road can be busy, but there are spots to leave your car along the southwest side of the bridge. The take out access is manageable at the north east corner of the bridge. There is a bit of challenge getting gear up the banks, but it is definitely worth it. Scout your take out from the bridge before heading to the put in.

Directions to Put In

Go back (west) on Rt 96 0.3 miles to the intersection with
     Rt 46.

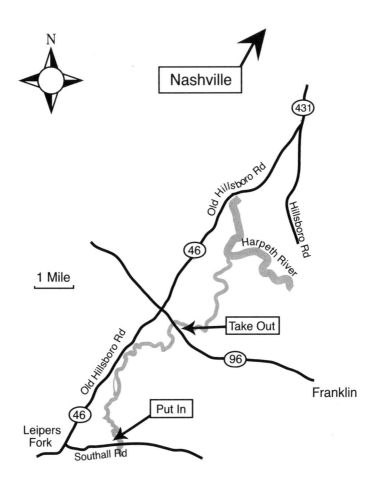

West Harpeth

Leipers Fork to Hwy 96

Paddle #25

Turn left (south) onto Rt 46.
Continue on Rt 46 for 4.3 miles to Southall Rd.
Turn left (east) on Southall Rd.
Continue on Southall Rd for 1.4 miles to bridge over water.

Put In Access

Parking along the side of the bridge is questionable, but 0.5 miles further east is a spacious parking lot of a church. Inquire about leaving your car here after dropping off boats and gear at the bridge. Put in is quite manageable and a little adventurous at the northwest corner of the bridge after sliding equipment down the embankment.

Interesting Points Along the Trip

There is a very remote feel to the stream as one starts out this trip, which may be in part from the high tree lined banks and the low density of development in this area. An amazing number of birds are around to serenade your paddle. We spotted an owl, hawk and a great blue heron. Near the Boyd Mill Rd Bridge is an impressive wall of stacked stone, the remains of the Boyd Mill.

Precautions

As always, strainers and deadfalls need to be dealt with; be especially careful where the waterway is narrow. There are some sections of faster water, but for the most part, this is a mild run.

Total Length

This trip is 5.7 miles, which takes about 3 hours to paddle.

Season

This section runs well in spring. In a dry summer, you will have to drag the boats in the shallow areas. Natural debris high along the banks is evidence that in wet seasons there is significant water flowing here.

Map

TN Atlas Map 36

The remains of the Boyd Mill

Bledsoe Creek

Paddle #26 Rogana Road to Old Union Access

Bledsoe Creek is in Sumner County and runs into the Cumberland River, where it is known as Old Hickory Lake. The four miles closest to Cumberland River can be paddled, but it does have a channel over 15 feet deep and is used by motorboats too. The next 5.5 miles up, however, are for the paddler. Bob Lantz in his book on Tennessee Rivers notes that this creek with class 2 rapids is best run when water levels are high. Having run this when water levels were low and ending up getting out of our boats hundreds of times to pull them over rocky shoals I would have to agree with him. The creek flows on a slippery rock bed, which makes dragging the boats an added challenge. This creek is beautiful and when flowing well has numerous riffles, gentle rapids as well as the above noted class 2 rapid and swimming holes. The banks and ledge are lined with only a few signs of civilization.

Directions to Take Out

From Nashville, head east on Interstate 40.
Take Interstate 40 to Exit 232 B north for Gallatin (Rt 109).
Proceed north on Rt 109 for 12.8 miles to the light at
    Airport Rd.
Turn right (east) on Airport Rd.
Continue on Airport Rd for 3.8 miles to the light for Rt 25
    (Hartsville Pike).
Turn right (east) onto Hartsville Pike/Rt 25.
Proceed on Rt 25 for 3.2 miles.
Just before the bridge going over Bledsoe Creek turn right
    (south) into the Old Union Access area.

Take Out Access

The parking area here is paved and the boat ramp makes for a very convenient take out. Since it is just south of the Rt 25 bridge going over Bledsoe Creek it is very easy to spot on your return trip.

Directions to Put In

Back to Rt 25 and turn right (east) crossing over
    Bledsoe Creek.
Continue east on Rt 25 for 0.6 mile to Greenfield Lane.
Turn left (north) onto Greenfield Lane.
Proceed north on Greenfield Lane for 3.5 miles to Rogana Rd.
Make a sharp left on Rogana Rd and continue for 0.8 mile.
Just prior to the bridge going over Bledsoe Creek are some
    parking spots.

Put in Access

At the bridge, there is a steep put in, but prior to the bridge along Rogana Rd is a pull off area with a cleared easy entry path to the creek.

Interesting Points along the Trip

This section of the Bledsoe Creek can be fast moving and exciting (depending on water level) with a class 2 rapid as the creek flows over some ledge drops about half way down the trip. The water is clear, much of it running over a solid rock bed. Numerous schools of fish can be seen swimming in the clear water.

Precautions

Watch for strainers, class 2 rapids and slippery rock when

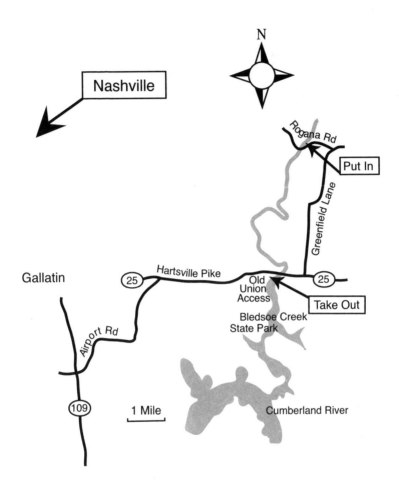

Bledsoe Creek

Rogana Rd to Old Union Access

Paddle #26

walking in creek.

Total Length

Total length of this trip is 5.5 miles which can take from 3 hours when the water is running to 5 hours when dry and walking across the shoals becomes part of the adventure.

Season

This trip is water dependent so it is best in winter and spring.

Map

TN Atlas Map 54

Dragging boats along in Bledsoe Creek

Sycamore Creek

Paddle #27 Water Plant Road to Bridge on Route 12

The lively stream for this trip runs through Cheatham county in a southwest direction into the Cumberland River. The strainers and deadfalls make it a challenging fun run.

Directions to Take out

From Nashville, head northwest to Ashland City via Rt 12 (Ashland City Hwy).
In downtown Ashland City watch for the intersection of Rt 49 and Rt 12.
Set your odometer here and continue on Rt 12 for 5 miles.
Here you pass over the Sycamore Creek.
Take the first right onto Macon Wall Rd and turn onto the dirt road immediately on the right which leads to the river.

Take out Access

The take out just before the bridge is very convenient as you can drive right up to the landing.

Put In

Return to Macon Wall Rd and left (southeast) onto Rt 12.
Take Rt 12 for 5 miles to Ashland City and the intersection of Rt 49.
At Rt 49, turn left (northeast).
Proceed on Rt 49 for 3.8 miles to Water Plant Rd, which is next to a bridge crossing Sycamore Creek.
Turn right (east) onto Water Plant Rd and park here.

Put in Access

The incline here involves a little maneuvering but is manageable. Watch out for poison ivy.

Interesting Points Along the Trip

In early spring, there are an amazing number of wild flowers along the banks of the Sycamore. Watch for bluebells, spring beauties, violets and red bud trees. In the early part of the trip, you cross under a swinging footbridge. This is a connector for parts of Girl Scout land. If you are interested in trying it out, be sure to ask ahead of time.

Precautions

Be on the lookout for deadfalls and strainers. The number of deadfalls and the currents creates an opportunity for lots of steering practice. In places, the only option is to get out and portage the boat around fallen trees.

Total Length of Trip

This trip is 6.3 miles, which, at a leisurely pace, takes 3 to 4 hours.

Season
This trip is best made between January and May or following heavy rains.

Map

TN Atlas 52

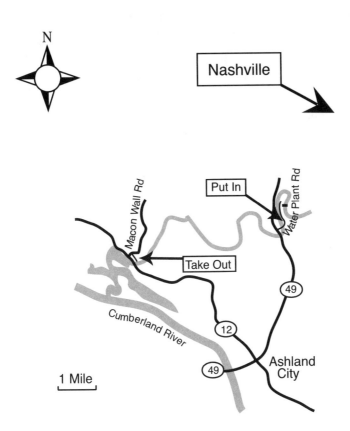

Sycamore Creek

Water Plant Road to Bridge on Route 12

Paddle #27

Turnbull Creek

Paddle #28 Highway 96 to Ulrich Landing Park

This creek twists and turns in a northeast direction from Dickson county to the Harpeth River in Cheatham county. While this is a long run, its beauty through farmlands and along high cliffs keeps it interesting and its feisty action keeps one challenged.

Directions to Take Out

From Nashville, take Interstate 40 west to Exit #188, Kingston Springs Rt 249.
At exit stop sign, go right for 0.2 miles to stop light.
At stoplight, turn left (west) onto West Kingston Springs Rd (not Rt 249).
Continue on West Kingston Springs Rd for 1.4 miles to 3-way stop sign.
Turn left (west) at the stop sign, still on West Kingston Springs Rd.
Continue on West Kingston Springs Rd for 1 mile to bridge.
Here, bear left (rather than taking bridge over RR tracks).
Stay along the Turnbull Creek for 0.5 miles to Ulrich Landing Park.
Ulrich Landing Park is on the left. Park here.

Take out access

Follow the path down to the creek. For the first trip, you will want to mark a river tree with some sort of sign to alert you to the end of your paddling trip. Currently, there are rocks on the side of the creek that make it a bit difficult to land here but going beyond the rocks to the stream that runs into the Turnbull provides a fairly easy exit.

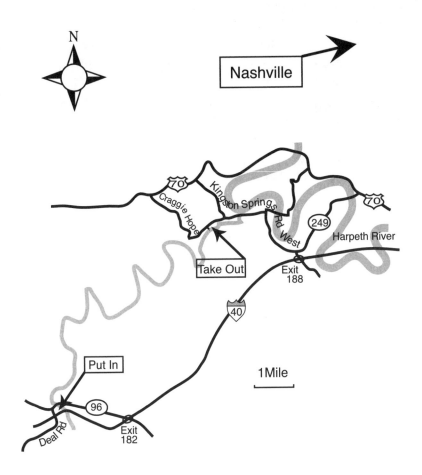

Turnbull Creek

Hwy 96 to Ulrich Landing Park

Paddle #28

Directions to Put in

Turn right out of the Ulrich Landing Park.
Go along the Turnbull Creek for 0.5 miles to the
   Kingston Springs Rd.
Continue straight ahead for 1 mile to the 3-way stop in
   Kingston Springs.
Turn right (southeast) onto West Kingston Springs Rd.
Proceed for 1.4 miles to traffic light and Rt 249.
Turn right (south) onto 249 for 0.2 miles to
   Interstate 40 West.
Take Interstate 40 West to Exit 182 Fairview
   Dickson Rt 96.
At exit light, turn left (west) on Rt 96 to Dickson.
Continue on Rt 96 for 2 miles to Deal Rd (after
   bridge over Turnbull Creek).
Turn left on Deal Rd and then left to parking area
   on left.

Put in Access

Unload here and carry boats down the path to the river.
There are a few places to put in at the end of this path. If
you want to catch the fast water at the base of the trail, just
carry your boat a bit further upstream to any available sandbar or opening onto the creek.

Interesting Points Along the Trip

As this creek twists and turns in a generally northeastly
manner, you pass alongside a number of impressive cliffs,
some with gentle waterfalls. A few of these cliffs must offer
enticing air currents as hawks and buzzards are usually
seen soaring above. The creek has some fun channels for
the paddler and a few chutes. Most of the land along this
creek is undeveloped or farmland so there is an abundance

of wildlife and beautiful wild flowers.

Precautions

Numerous deadfalls and lively currents make this stream adventurous.

Total Length - Distance

The trip is 11.5 miles, which takes about 6 hours to paddle.

Season

Running this creek is dependent on water level. It is best in late fall, winter and early spring – especially after a good rain.

Map of River TN Atlas Map 52

Rocky Cliffs above the Turnbull Creek

Jones Creek

Paddle #29 Jones Creek Road to Petty Road

Jones Creek meanders through Dickson county, flowing in a northeastern direction to join the Harpeth River. We were cautioned that this creek runs low, and we would probably have to drag our boats in places. However, we made this trip in the spring and were able to navigate the whole trip on running water. The area is pristine, with the beautiful Tennessee countryside for scenery. Rocky bluffs abound along the way with plenty of wild flowers (in season) and wildlife. The pools of crystal clear water offer the fisherman, as well as the swimmer, ideal sporting spots.

Directions to Take Out

Head west out of Nashville on Interstate 40.
Exit Interstate 40 at Mc Cory Lane exit #192.
Turn right (north) at the end of the exit ramp onto
    McCrory Lane.
Continue on McCrory Lane for 1.2 miles where McCrory
    Lane ends on US 70.
Turn left (west) onto US 70 and continue for 13.5 miles.
In White Bluff at the intersection Rt 47, turn right (north).
Proceed north on Rt 47 for 2.2 miles.
Bear right onto Rt 250.
Proceed on Rt 250 for 0.8 miles to Petty Rd.
Turn left (west) onto Petty Rd.
Continue on Petty Rd for 4 miles to the bridge over
    Jones Creek.

Take Out Access

Leave vehicle on shoulder of road by bridge. There are

Jones Creek

Jones Creek Rd to Petty Rd

Paddle #29

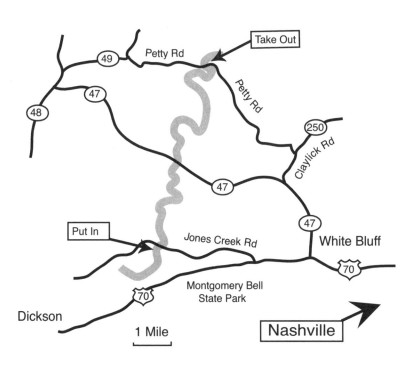

some potential parking spots on the southwest corner of the bridge. However, when getting out of the river, the northeast corner seems the easiest for getting the boats up to the road. Check out the exit options prior to running the river so you know which you prefer. On the southwest corner of the bridge, there is a small creek coming into the Jones Creek. Just beyond this little creek is an area to head up the hill to the bridge on Petty Rd.

Directions for Put In

Retrace steps back to US 70 by
    heading back east 4 miles on Petty Rd to Hwy 250.
Turn right (south) onto Hwy 250.
Go south on Hwy 250 for 0.8 miles to Hwy 47.
Turn left (south) onto Hwy 47 toward White Bluff.
South on Hwy 47 for 2.2 miles to the Intersection of US 70.
Turn right (west) on US 70.
Proceed west on US 70 for 1.3 miles to Jones Creek Rd.
At Jones Creek Rd, turn right (northwest).
Proceed on Jones Creek Rd for 2.7 miles to the bridge over
    the creek.

Put In Access

There are places to leave your car alongside the Jones Creek Rd Bridge. Access is possible from more than one spot but is easiest from the southwest corner of the bridge. Just slide the boats down the hill and off you go.

Interesting Points Along the Trip

Numerous ripples make this a peppy stream. With the ever-present deadfalls, one must stay alert and paddle conscientiously. The rocky cliffs add to the visual beauty of the trip, but most beautiful is the creek itself. The water runs clear and in some pools is a startling blue. There are also some interesting rock formations that the creek runs over. Note the variation of rock in the beginning of the trip. You will pass under two bridges, as well as by the remains of an old stacked stone bridge, before coming to the Petty Creek Rd Bridge.

Precautions

Keep alert for deadfalls, strainers and ripples. Rumor also has it that barbwire is occasionally out to keep cattle from roaming too far from home via the creek.

Total Length

This segment of the Jones Creek is 8 miles, which can take around 4 to 5 hours depending on stops and water flow.

Season

In spring, there is enough water for this section. In dry weather, you may have to drag your boat.

Map TN Atlas Map 52

Waterfalls into Jones Creek

Jones Creek

Paddle #30 Petty Road to Timber Ridge Road

Jones Creek maintains its pristine beauty along this stretch of the creek. Scenery is spectacular in spots, with high rocky bluffs placed alongside the clear water creek. This section is a tad more adventurous and remote, with no roadside noise from put in to take out.

Directions to Take Out

Head west from Nashville on Interstate 40.
Exit Interstate 40 at McCrory Lane (exit # 192).
Turn right (north) at the end of the exit ramp onto McCrory Lane.
Continue on McCrory Lane for 1.2 miles where McCrory Lane ends on US 70.
Turn left (west) onto US 70 and continue for 13.5 miles.
In White Bluff, at the intersection of US 70 and Rt 47, turn right (north west).
Continue on Rt 47 for 9.5 miles to the junction of Rt 48.
Turn right (north) on Rt 48.
Go on Rt 48 for a short 0.4 miles to Rt 49 in Charlotte.
Turn right (north east) onto Rt 49.
Proceed on Rt 49 for 7.3 miles to Timber Ridge Rd.
Turn right (east) onto Timber Ridge Rd.
Proceed on Timber Ridge for 3.7 miles to the low water crossing over Jones Creek.

Take Out Access

There is limited space to leave a car at the far side of the low water crossing, but take out is very convenient, with the road at creek side.

Jones Creek

Petty Rd to Timber Ridge Rd

Paddle # 30

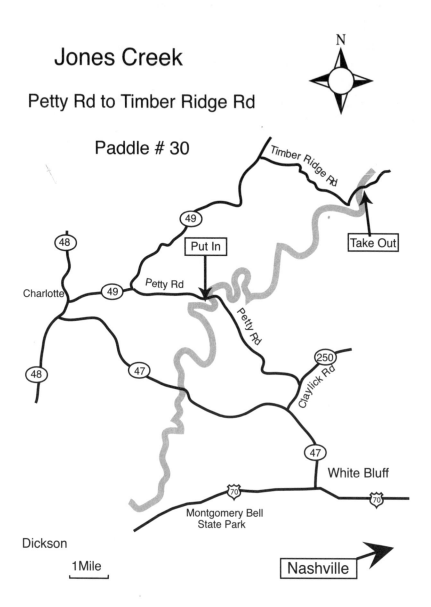

N

Timber Ridge Rd

49

Put In

48

49

Petty Rd

Charlotte

Petty Rd

Take Out

250

Claylick Rd

48

47

47

White Bluff

70

Montgomery Bell
State Park

70

Dickson

1 Mile

Nashville

121

Directions to Put In

Head back out Timber Ridge Rd (now west) for 3.7 miles
 to Rt 49.
Turn left (south) on Rt 49.
Proceed on Rt 49 for 5.6 miles to Petty Rd.
Turn left onto Petty Rd.
Proceed on Petty Rd for 2.1 miles to bridge over
 Jones Creek.

Put In Access

There are parking spaces on the shoulder of the road on
either side of the bridge. The creek can be entered from
either side, but we found sliding the boats down on the
southwest corner worked well.

Interesting Points Along the Trip

Natural beauty abounds along the Jones Creek. There are
plenty of rocky island beaches for picnics and pools of deep
water for swimming and fishing. We were warned of a
major drop shortly after entering the water at the first bend,
but instead found a fun little rapid shoot. It could be that the
spring rains allowed for more water than usual so the pool-
ing below the rocky drop wasn't too extreme. Anyway, with
the spring water, this section of the Jones was moving at a
pleasant pace and offering numerous challenges for the
conservative adventurer.

Precautions

Again, stay alert for deadfalls, strainers and large rocks.
We did have to portage around one fallen tree on this trip
and navigate around numerous deadfalls. Also, stay alert
for barbed wire as it is used by some cattle farmers to keep
control of the livestock and gets pretty close to the creek.

Watch for a ledge drop of a foot or two, fairly close to the end of the route.

Total Length

The length of this trip is about 8.8 miles, which can take 4 to 5 hours, depending on stops, paddling and water flow.

Season

In spring, there is plenty of water for this section. It is especially fun with the water running fast.

Map

TN Atlas Map 52

Little people fishing along the creek.

Yellow Creek

Paddle #31 Route 13 to
Route 149 Wildlife Refuge Area

This paddle north of Nashville near Clarksville offers a distinctly different experience from a number of other creeks in the area. As one starts out on this creek, it is small and fast moving with the challenges of navigating around strainers and deadfalls. After McFall Rd Bridge, the creek widens and slows considerably to the point where you feel you are paddling in a lake. In fact, the creek is flowing into the Cumberland where it is Lake Barkley so this is to be expected. Prior to the take out, one comes to the Tennessee Wildlife Refuge (TWRA), so there is usually an abundance of wildlife in the area. The TWRA land is also good for hiking, but be cautious in hunting season.

Directions to Take Out

From Nashville, take Interstate 24 North to Exit 11
    Clarksville 76 west.
Proceed on Rt 76 west for 3.3 miles to traffic light
    where Rt 76 changes the name of the road to Alt 41
    BYP(bypass) North.
Continue straight ahead onto Alt 41 BYP North (76/12)
    (don't turn onto 41).
Continue on Alt 41 BYP North for 5.5 miles to Rt 13.
Turn left (south) on Rt 13.
Take Rt 13 for 2.5 miles to Rt 149 West.
Turn right (west) onto Rt 149.
Proceed on Rt 149 for 11.9 miles to bridge over
    Yellow Creek.
Just past the Yellow Creek Bridge turn left onto
    Old Hwy 149 and the parking lot for recreational use.

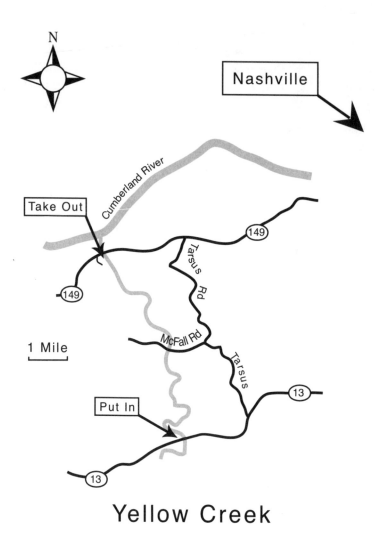

Yellow Creek

Rt 13 to Rt 149 Wildlife Refuge Area

Paddle #31

Take Out Access

The boat ramp here makes this an easy access. The bridge over the creek will make the area very identifiable for the return trip. There are paths off the parking lot that are part of the TWRA land and available for hiking. Be aware though that hunting is permitted here from September through January.

Directions to Put In

Out of the parking lot, turn right on Rt 149 heading east.
Proceed on Rt 149 east for 2.5 miles to Tarsus Rd.
Turn right (south) onto Tarsus Rd.
Continue on Tarsus Rd for 6.1 miles until it ends on Rt 13.
Turn right (west) on Rt 13.
Take Rt 13 for 2 miles to the bridge over the Yellow Creek.

Put In Access

Parking is available just off the road on the right or left, west of the bridge. There is a car path going down to the water on the north side, so it is convenient for unloading boats and equipment. A sandbar makes an easy access to the water.

Interesting Points along the Trip

The first five miles before McFall Rd are lively with sandbars and swimming holes in clear blue water. After McFall Rd bridge, the water will slow down and take on a swamp-like appearance. The TRWA land to the left of the creek ensures an abundance of wildlife in the area.

Precautions

There are deadfalls and strainers,and sometimes portaging
your boat is a necessity.

Total Length

This trip is 8.1 miles. This may take 4 to 5 hours to paddle,
as the last section is very slow.

Variation on the route

You can take out (or put in) at the McFall Rd Bridge.
McFall Rd is off of Tarsus Rd halfway between Rt 149 and
Rt 13. Either section of this paddle is about 4 miles. The
southern section is a faster paddle than the northern section
because of water currents.

Season This trip can be paddled all year

Map TN Atlas Map 51

Stray dogs along for a swim

Big Swan

Paddle #32 Natchez Trace Parkway to Horse Branch Road

In a wet season, this is a great stretch of adventure paddling. The creek twists and turns through rural Tennessee, offering clear water, occasional waterfalls on the side, tree lined banks, wildflowers, cows, water critters and birds aplenty. If you don't mind the sometime necessary portaging around deadfalls that completely block the creek, this is a wonderful adventure in a beautiful area. The outing begins right off the Natchez Trace Parkway at the bridge passing over the Big Swan. The Park Ranger says this is a good use of recreational land. He suggests unloading boats on the side of the road here and carrying them the short portage down the hill to the creek. You can then drive your car the half mile up the hill and leave it at the parking lot for Fall Hollow. After paddling, it's worth the short walk from the parking lot to check out the cascading waterfalls that feed into the Big Swan Creek at Fall Hollow.

Directions to Take Out

From Nashville, head south on the Natchez Trace Pky.
Proceed on Natchez Trace Parkway for 50 miles.
Exit at Rt 412, heading west toward Hohenwald.
Stay on Rt 412 for 2.1 miles to Salem Rd.
Turn right (north) on Salem Rd.
At 1.2 miles, cross over bridge and bear right.
At this point, the road is called Indian Creek Rd.
Further north this road changes its name to Swan Creek Rd.
From this bridge, it is 3.8 miles to Horse Branch Rd.
Take a right (east) onto Horse Branch Rd (the Big Swan is
    visible immediately).
Parking is available for your take out car along the road by
    the low water crossing.

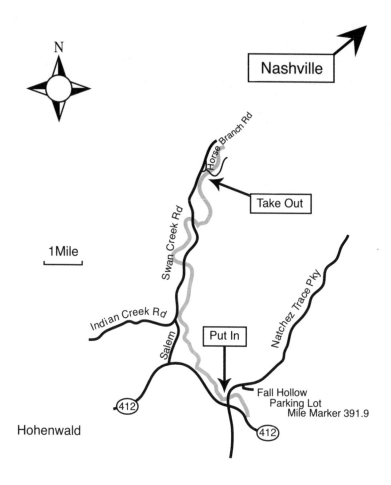

Big Swan Creek

Natchez Trace Parkway to Horse Branch Road

Paddle #32

Take Out Access

The take out is easily recognizable as you are paddling north. The low water crossing will necessitate your getting out of the creek before the bridge, and you can't miss the car on the side of the bridge. This is a flat, easy take out.

Directions to Put In

Go back up Horse Branch Road to Swan Creek Rd.
Turn left (south) onto Swan Creek Rd.
Continue south on Swan Creek Rd for 3.8 miles to bridge.
Cross the bridge bearing left (rather than going down Indian
    Creek Rd).
At this point, road is Salem Rd.
In 1 mile, Salem Rd ends on Rt 412.
Turn left (west) onto Rt 412.
Proceed on Rt 412 for 2.1 miles.
Turn onto Natchez Trace Pky, heading north to Nashville.
Within 0.5 miles, you will see the bridge over the
    Big Swan Creek.

Put In Access

Unload boats at the northwest corner of bridge, and it is a short easy slide down to the creek. From here, take your car to the Fall Hollow Parking lot. This is at mile 391.9 on the Natchez Trace Parkway. Park here and it's less than a 0.5 mile walk to the put in where all your gear awaits.

Interesting Points Along the Trip

This is a beautiful paddle through rural woodlands and farmland. The water is crystal clear, offering views of under-water life and opportunities to cool off. Wildlife we've spotted include muskrat and beaver. Birds sing along the way. Besides the Great Blue Heron, which seems to lead all TN creek paddles, there are green heron and kingfishers. Waterfalls can be spotted along the way. When hearing the sound of cascading water, look into the brush for the water-falls, as there are a number of them in the wet seasons. Wildflowers dot the shores in season.

Precautions

There are many deadfalls and strainers as this is not a heavily traveled route. At certain spots there is no choice but to get out and portage in the woods around deadfalls.

Total Length

The trip is 7.5 miles which takes about 4 hours.

Season

The season is water dependent. In wet summers, we have done this in August, but in dry summers water level may be too low. The trip is best in spring and winter.

Map of River TN Atlas Map 35

On a hot day, it is not unusual to find cows cooling off.

Big Swan Creek

Paddle #33 Horse Branch Road to Raleigh Chapel Road

This stretch of the Big Swan Creek is beautiful and very entertaining, with numerous deadfalls and strainers. There are navigational challenges all along the route, interspersed with sparkling blue water swimming holes and gravel bars for the occasional rest. The landscape is pastoral Tennessee at its best with cattle alongside the river and birds galore. The area is rich in wildlife and wild flowers.

Directions to Take Out

From Nashville, head south on the Natchez Trace Parkway.
Proceed on the Natchez Trace Parkway for 34 miles.
Exit Natchez Trace Parkway at mile marker 408
    for Centerville (Jct Rt 50 West).
Proceed on Route 50, west for 11.5 miles.
Turn left (south) on to Swan Creek Rd.
Continue on Swan Creek Road for 1.3 miles.
Turn left (east) onto Raleigh Chapel Rd.
Continue on Raleigh Chapel Rd for 1.3 miles until you
    arrive at the bridge crossing the Big Swan Creek.

Take Out Access

Since this site is at a low water crossing, which you can't go under, there is no danger of passing by the take out on the return trip. It also assures easy maneuvering to get your boat out of the water, as there is hardly any incline on the bank of the river. Getting the boat back to the car is an easy transport. There are a few spots for parking before and after the bridge on the side of the road.

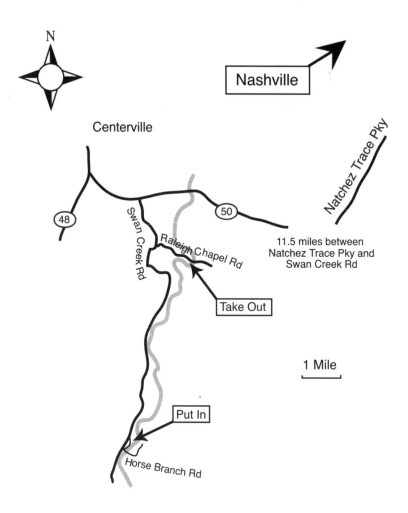

Big Swan Creek

Horse Branch Rd to Raleigh Chapel Rd

Paddle #33

Directions to Put In

Return back on Raleigh Chapel Road 1.3 miles to Swan
    Creek Road.
Go left (south) on Swan Creek Road for 6.4 miles to
    Horse Branch Rd.
Turn left (east) onto Horse Branch Road.
Horse Branch Road crosses the Big Swan Creek
    almost immediately.

Put In Access

As Horse Branch Road crosses the Big Swan Creek with a
low water crossing, the access is easy. Parking is conve-
niently located along the road by the bridge.

Interesting Points along the Trip

Lots of Middle Tennessee beauty exists along this stretch of
the creek: wildflowers, birds, rock formations, wildlife, crystal
clear water and blue water swimming holes.

Precautions

Deadfalls and strainers are the main concerns when paddling the Big Swan Creek. There are places where portaging your boat is a necessity, and places where it may be
wise, depending on your navigational skills.

Total Length

This trip is 6.7 miles long and takes about 3 to 4 hours.

Variations

If you want a shorter trip, you can get off at the Peery Bend Road Bridge, which is visible from Swan Creek Rd. This road is located 4.5 miles south of Rt 50 and 3.2 miles north of Horse Branch Rd. The distance for this segment between Horse Branch Rd and Peery Bend Bridge is about 5 miles. Parking is available by the southwest corner of the bridge with a path to a gravel bar take out.

Season

The season is water dependent. This can be done in wet summers and falls. It is a good trip for spring and winter.

Map of the River

TN Atlas Map 35

Sit-on-top Ocean kayaks meet Tennessee.

Big Swan

Paddle #34 Raleigh Chapel Rd to the Duck River

This stretch of the Big Swan is rarely paddled, judging from the number of deadfalls, but fun and full of adventure. From Raleigh Chapel north, there are no access points until joining the Duck River, so one has the feeling of being in a very remote area. The creek twists and turns, offering numerous choices in paths as you head to the river. On our last trip, we did have to portage around or over deadfalls three times. While this wouldn't be good for beginners, it does add to the sense of adventure. The creek is snappy, clear and clean. Most banks are tree lined, with the occasional cliff and waterfall offering its serenity.

Directions to Take Out

From Nashville, head south on the Natchez Trace Parkway to mile marker 408.
At exit of Natchez Trace, turn right (west to Centerville) on Rt 50.
Stay on Rt 50 for 13 miles to where Rt 50 joins Rt 48 and Rt 100.
Go right (north) on Rt 48/100 through the town,Centerville.
Go around the town square, continuing on Rt 48/100 North (total distance on Rt 48 Rt 100 is 1.6 miles).
Before crossing the bridge over the Duck River, turn left into the city park (soccer nets visible from road) and find a parking space.

Take Out Access

There is a nice ramp going down to the water, so the portage is minimal. The take out is easily recognizable on the return trip as it is after the bridge on the Duck River.

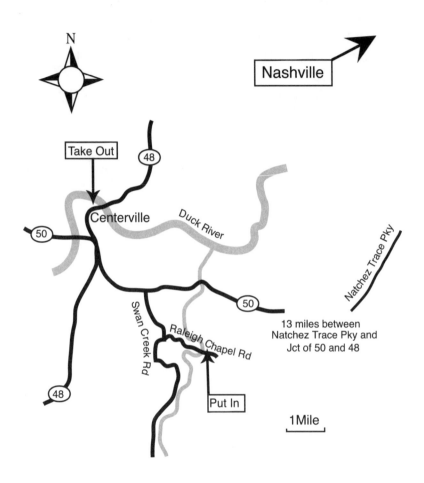

Big Swan Creek

Raleigh Chapel Rd to the Duck River

Paddle #34

Directions to Put In

Turn right (southwest) out of the parking lot onto Rt 48/100.
Go for 1.6 miles on Rt 48/100 to Rt 50.
Turn left (east) onto Rt 50.
Continue on Rt 50 for 1.5 miles to Swan Creek Rd.
Turn right (south) onto Swan Creek Rd.
Continue on Swan Creek Rd for 1.3 miles to Raleigh
    Chapel Rd.
Turn left (east) onto Raleigh Chapel Rd.
Continue on Raleigh Chapel Rd for 1.3 miles to the low
    water crossing of the Big Swan Creek and put in area.

Put In Access

The northeast corner of the bridge has a flat gravel area
adjacent to the river, so put in is easy. Parking is available
alongside the bridge and creek. Some places are posted.

Interesting Points along the Trip

Heavily tree lined banks provide shade and beauty for
this paddle. The water is crystal clear, with pools available
for swimming. Waterfalls can be spotted along the rocky
cliffs that hide behind trees. Wildlife and flowers are every-
where. The trip is varied, from the snappy pace of the creek
for the first half of the trip, to the slow meandering of the
Duck River

Precautions

Frequent deadfalls across the whole creek necessitate
portages out of the water around obstacles. The stream
splits in a number of places, some paths being better than
others, but that's for you to explore. The current at places
has to be watched to avoid being pulled to the strainers.

Total Length

The trip is a total of 6.8 miles of which 3.4 miles are on the Swan Creek and 3.4 miles are on the Duck River. This can take 3 to 5 hours to paddle.

Season

The season is water dependent. We have done this in summer, but most reliably floatable in winter, spring and late fall.

Map

Tn Atlas Map 35

Giant rootball on deadfall

Fortyeight Creek
Paddle # 35 Fortyeight Creek Rd to the Buffalo River

This creek, located southwest of Hohenwald, has its own unique beauty. The water is clear, flowing over massive rock formations with blue swimming holes at respectable intervals. Woodlands, pastures and rocky cliffs adorn the banks of this remote creek. By nature, this waterway is narrow, and the deadfalls will keep you on the alert as you paddle away. This is not a leisurely paddle due to the maneuvering that needs to be done, but it is a fun workout. Watch out for barbed wire strung across the creek, intended to keep cattle from roaming but dangerous for the paddler.

Directions to Take Out

Head south on the Natchez Trace Parkway.
Go southwest on the Natchez Trace Parkway for 50.5 miles.
Exit at mile marker 392 for Rt 412.
At stop sign, turn left (west) for Hohenwald.
Stay on 412 for 8 miles to Hohenwald.
At intersection of Rt 412 and Rt 48 turn left (south)
    onto Rt 48.
Continue on route 48 for 8.7 miles to Topsy Rd
    (note sign for Topsy Canoe and Camp).
Turn left (south) onto Topsy Rd.
Stay on Topsy Rd for 4.8 miles.
After the Topsy Turvey Canoe Co, bear left onto the gravel
    road just prior to the Topsy Bridge.

Take Out Access

The gravel road at the northeast corner of the bridge offers a number of parking spots and a short, cleared carry to the river. This spot is on the Buffalo River and you will be

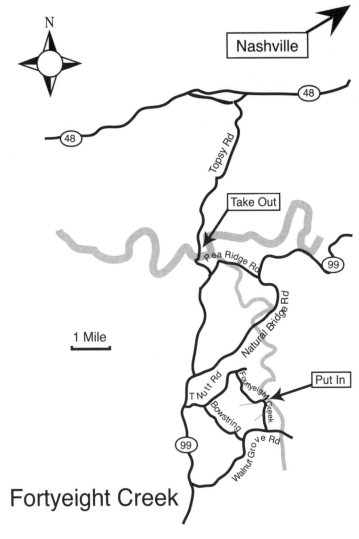

Fortyeight Creek

Fortyeight Creek Rd to the Buffalo River

Paddle #35

able to identify it as the first bridge after Fortyeight Creek joins the Buffalo River. This is less than a mile after the confluence. The spot is popular among fishermen.

Directions to Put In

Return out the gravel road, turn left (south) and go over the
  bridge.
Continue on Topsy Rd for 0.8 miles to Pea Ridge Rd.
Turn left (east) onto Pea Ridge Rd.
Proceed on Pea Ridge for 1.6 miles where it ends on Rt 99.
Turn right (south) onto Rt 99.
Continue on Rt 99 for 4.8 miles (note Spa) to T Nutt Rd.
Turn left onto T Nutt Rd.
Proceed on T Nutt Rd for 0.5 miles to Bowstring Rd.
Turn right onto Bowstring Rd.
Continue on Bowstring Rd for 1.4 miles to Walnut Grove Rd.
Turn left onto Walnut Grove Rd.
Go on Walnut Grove Rd 0.6 miles to Fortyeight Creek Rd.
Turn left onto Fortyeight Creek Rd.
Continue on Fortyeight Creek Rd for 0.8 miles.
Turn right and park along creek at 0.4 miles.

Put In Access

A small stream runs across the road here so it is easy to just pull the boats into the creek from the road.   There are a number of parking spots along this gravel road.

Interesting Points Along the Trip

This run is most notable for keeping one alert to paddling conditions. Between the deadfalls, strainers and turns in the creek, you have to pay attention to where you want to be and then get there. However, there is enough time to enjoy the scenery, which is beautiful. There are plenty of rock formations along the banks, as well as under water formations, which are quite intriguing. The water is clear, so fish viewing is easy. Birds and wildlife abound. Along this stretch is a natural bridge, however, it is on private land and the owners dammed up the creek here, making it difficult to locate. If you stop at the Tennessee Spa and ask they may be willing to let you have a look. It is definitely an amazing wonder of nature and worth inquiring about.

Precautions

Keep alert for deadfalls and strainers, especially in narrow passageways. Also, be aware that some farmers string barbed wire across the creek to keep their cattle from wandering away.

Total Length

This trip is 6.8 miles, which can take 4 to 5 hours. Be sure to allow time to check out the natural bridge.

Resource Number

Topsy Turvy Canoe Rental and Campground: 931-722-3530. Besides renting canoes and having a campground, these folks offer shuttle service if you have your own boat and only one car. Call ahead.

Season

Water levels are low in summer. This run is best in late fall, winter and spring.

Map TN Atlas Map 19

Cane Creek

Paddle #36 Farmers Exchange to Pleasantville

This truly beautiful section of Cane Creek should be run when there is plenty of water. In summer, we had a fair amount of dragging to do in the shallow spots, but the beauty of the area made it worth it. Also, there are numerous clear blue swimming holes and fish galore. On one trip, we met an old fisherman who told of a hidden cave in one of the bluffs. We didn't find the cave but were impressed with overhanging cliffs, and gentle falls of water.

Directions to Take Out

Head south from Nashville on the Natchez Trace Parkway.
Exit the Natchez Trace at Rt 50 (south of mile marker 408).
Take a right off the ramp toward Centerville on Rt 50 West.
Continue on Rt 50 W for 13.2 miles to Rt 100/Rt 48.
At the intersection of Rt 100/Rt 48 turn left
    (west and south).
Stay on Rt 100 West for 17.5 miles to Cane Creek Rd.
At Cane Creek Rd, turn left (south) for 0.3 miles.
There is parking just past the guardrail.

Take Out Access

There is a wide worn path from the road down to the creek. However, at the end of the float, the spot can be easy to miss. Be sure to identify the area so you don't go past it. There is a slight incline from the creek to the road, but it is easy to deal with.

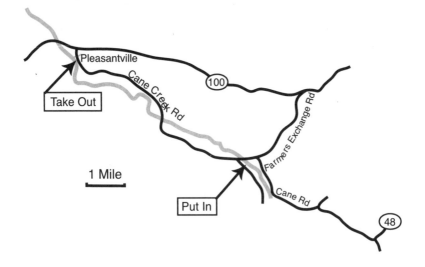

Cane Creek

Farmers Exchange to Cane Creek Rd
in Pleasantville

Paddle #36

Directions to Put In

Continue down Cane Creek Rd (south east) for 5.6 miles
    to the second bridge over the Cane Creek.
Turn right just before this bridge, as there are parking spots
    here along the creek.

Put In Access

From the southwest corner of the bridge, there is a gentle sloping path to the water.

Interesting Points along the Trip

Most interesting along this section of the Cane Creek is
the overhanging ledge of rock. If the water isn't too high,
you can paddle beneath it.   There are a number of rocky
bluffs along the paddle, and we were told of a cave in one of
them. The water of the Cane Creek is crystal clear and
offers numerous swimming holes.

Precautions

Strainers and deadfalls are plentiful, so be on the out-
look. Be prepared to do some portaging around deadfalls
that go all the way across the creek. If the water level is low
there may be some dragging necessary.

Season

This run is best when there is plenty of water, so usually
good in spring, late fall, and winter.

Total Length

The length of this trip is about 6.2 miles. This can be paddled in 3 to 4 hours, depending on water flow and stops.

Map

TN Atlas Map 35

Rocky bluffs along the Cane Creek

Cane Creek

Paddle #37 Pleasantville Off Hwy 100
to Off Hwy 438

This section of Cane Creek, which is in Hickman county, offers great creek paddling. Its location is remote, which is good if you like to be alone in a beautiful spot. However, there isn't anyone coming by to remove deadfalls, so that means lots of portaging around or over the deadfalls. The water level may be low in places, so there can be a bit of dragging your boat. The trip is full of adventure with active paddling for the whole seven miles. The water is crystal clear with the blue water swimming holes of Middle Tennessee. At times, it feels as if you are paddling from one aquarium to another. The fish population in this area is amazing - from schools of minnows to big bass. If you like paddling and fishing, this may be the place to be.

Directions to Take Out

From Nashville, head southwest on Hwy 100.
As you cross the bridge over the Duck River on the
    approach to Centerville, start your odometer.
Continue west on Hwy 100 from here for 19.7 miles to
    Lower Cane Creek Rd.
Turn right (northwest) onto Lower Cane Creek Rd.
Continue on Lower Cane Creek Rd for 3.9 miles until it ends
    on Hwy 438.
Turn left (west) on Hwy 438.
Continue on Hwy 438 for 1.7 miles.
Turn right (north) here (no sign but bridge over the Cane
    Creek 0.1 miles north is visible from intersection).

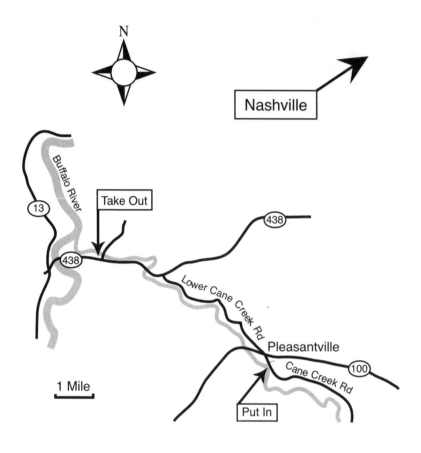

Cane Creek

Pleasantville off Hwy 100 to off Hwy 438

Paddle #37

Take Out Access

Parking is available along side the bridge. A good take out path exists on the southwest corner of the bridge, as well as good parking spots. When paddling, just go under the bridge and take out on river left. Note the bridge color for take out recognizability. There will be a short portage up the grassy embankment, but it isn't too strenuous.

Directions to Put In

Return to Hwy 438, turning left (east) onto Hwy 438.
Continue on Hwy 438 for 1.7 miles.
Turn right (east) onto Lower Cane Creek Rd.
Continue on Lower Cane Creek Rd for 3.8 miles.
Turn left (east) onto Hwy 100.
Go a short 0.1 miles to Cane Creek Rd.
Turn right (southeast) onto Cane Creek Rd.
Go 0.2 miles to just past the metal guardrails over a branch that feeds the Cane Creek.

Put In Access

Parking spots are available just beyond the guardrails, and a path here goes down to the Cane Creek. The down-hill nature of the path makes this an easy slide for the boats and equipment. The sandy, rocky bottom of the Cane Creek makes it an easy entry here.

Interesting Points along the Trip

This creek wanders through woodland and ranch country. The crystal clear nature of the water makes it a memorable run. While there is plenty of wildlife and wildflowers adorning the banks, the visible fish population is most remarkable. The swimming holes are numerous and appreciated on a hot day, given all the paddling one does maneuvering around in these waters.

Precautions

Deadfalls are the biggest safety concern, and one must portage around or over a number of them. The water level in dry seasons may be too low for heavily laden boats.

Total Length

This trip is 6.3 miles long which takes 3 to 4 hours to paddle.

Season

This run is water dependent. In wet summers, we have done this but it is best in winter, spring and late fall.

Map

TN Atlas Map 35

Maneuvering around deadfalls

References

Canoeing in Tennessee, Sherwin, Holly. Allpen Books Press, LLC, Mukilteo, WA. 2002

National Organization for Rivers, web site-www.nationalrivers.org for information on paddling, river conservation, access, and navigability law.

Paddling Asheville and Southern Appalachia, Mayers, Betsy. Betsy Mayers, 2004

Tennessee Atlas & Gazetteer, seventh Edition, DeLorme. 2004

Tennessee Rivers A Paddler's Guidebook, Lantz, Bob. The University of Tennessee Press 2003

Tennessee Scenic Rivers Association (TSRA), web site-www.paddletsra.org for information on schools, safety, trips and more.

TVA controlled flow information can be accessed at
    http://www.tva.com/river/lakeinfo
    or by phone at 800-238-2264